The Family Rashi Book

by

Shalom Hammer

DE❙**VORA**
PUBLISHING
JERUSALEM ◆ NEW YORK

The Family Rashi Book

Published by Devora Publishing Company
Text Copyright © 2010 Shalom Hammer

Cover Design: Shani Schmell
Typesetting: Ariel Walden
Editorial and Production Director: Daniella Barak
Editor: Sara Rosenbaum

Hard Cover ISBN: 978-1-934440-88-9
Soft Cover ISBN: 978-1-936068-16-6

First edition. Printed in Israel

Distributed by:

Urim Publications
POB 52287
Jerusalem 91521, Israel
Tel: 02.679.7633
Fax: 02.679.7634
urim_pub@netvision.net.il

Lambda Publishers, Inc.
527 Empire Blvd.
Brooklyn, NY 11225, USA
Tel: 718.972.5449
Fax: 781.972.6307
mh@ejudaica.com

www.UrimPublications.com

Dedication

To my parents

דוד יוסף בן יעקב יחיאל הלוי עמו״ש
פרידה רודה בת צירל עמו״ש

In their Honor and to their continued good health

הרב דוב בערל וויין

שדרות בן מימון 15, ירושלים 92262

Tevet 3 5770
20 December 2009

Rabbi Shalom Hammer is one of outstanding young rabbis and scholars here in Israel. He has already gained an international reputation for his speaking and writings. His latest work on Rashi and the Torah portions of the week is a boon to all Jewish families who wish to educate themselves and their children in an appreciation of the timeless words of the eternal teacher of Torah to Israel, Rashi. The book is user friendly and stimulating in its questions and insights. It is perfect for the Shabat table and for student reviews of lessons learned in school. In short, it is a marvelous addition to any Jewish home and will enhance family unity and knowledge.

May Rabbi Shalom Hammer be blessed to continue his great work on behalf of Torah and Israel.

With all blessings

Rabbi Berel Wein

In memory of our Aunt, Judy Leff
יהודית שרה בת אסתר,
who selflessly dedicated her life to being a מורה par excellence
to youngsters beginning their journey in the Torah world.
She helped her students develop a strong foundation
and love for Torah and yiddishkeit.

The Henzel Family

☙

In honor of my dear Mother, Nora נחמה רייזל,
and in loving memory of my late Father, Solly שאול.

Jonathan Tager

☙

In memory of my father, Solly Tager *z"l*
שאול בן אליהו זעליג הלוי ז"ל,
a man who epitomized what a real Jew is supposed to be
without all the external trappings and nonsense
which, unfortunately, often define a Jew today.
The only person I've ever – and almost certainly will ever –
come across who was worthy of the title Rebbe.

Robin, Trina, Leah, Adina, Shaul and Ben

☙

Rashi raised his daughters as scholars.
In honor of Gabrielle's Bat Mitzvah
we pray that our daughters, Alex, Gabrielle, Emily and Sophia
will also pursue scholarship and righteousness.
חכמת נשים בנתה ביתה

Michael and Drorit Ratzker

In honor of our children:
Ezra, Yona, Akiva and Tova.

Dr. Adam and Mrs. Shaani Splaver Hollywood Florida

ɕʎ

In memory of
אברהם לייב בן אריה לייביש ז״ל – ציפורה בת שמואל ז״ל
קתריאל בן יוסף מרדכי ז״ל – לאה בת שמחה ז״ל

Dr. Warren and Marlene Sobol

ɕʎ

In honor of my wife,
Rachel;
a true *aishes chayil*,
who has imbued her children with love for Hashem and humanity.

Dr. Jack Greenspan, Columbus Ohio

ɕʎ

In Honor of the Greenspan Family.

Scott, Karen, Shira and Ron Evans

In loving memory and לעילוי נשמת
Our Pop-Pop and Zaidie
נח יעקב בן יהושע ז"ל

Jeff, Sara, Ariella, Binyamin, Doniel, Shaiky and Yakir

❧

In loving memory of my grandpa, The Late Reverend Jossie Klitzner
הרב יוסף בן הרב נחום נתן
His path in Torah and Life inspires.

Saun and Yve Borstrock, Capetown, South Africa

❧

In honor of our parents,
Rabbi and Mrs. Sheldon Goldsmith,
Rabbi and Mrs. Bernard Stefansky,
who have instilled a love of learning in their children and grandchildren.

Bracha and Jonathan Stefansky

❧

Dedicated by
Andrew & Véronique Berman (London & Jerusalem)
in loving memory of
אליעזר בן אברהם ז"ל & אליקים יהודה בן מנחם צבי ז"ל
מאיר זאב בן אברהם בערל הלוי ז"ל & מיכאל בן בנימין ז"ל

All were proud supporters of Jewish life and identity
and were זוכה to see their grandchildren carry on their proud example.
"…but the crown of a good name surmounts them all." (אבות ד:יג)

CONTENTS

FOREWORD

"Rashi" is an acronym for the name Rabbi Shlomo Yitzchaki, but the Jewish tradition tells us it also stands for "*rebbe shel Yisrael*" – the teacher of the Jewish people. Rashi occupies a unique place in the Jewish world because he systematically provided the Jewish people with the tools to understand and analyze the text of the Torah.

By the time Rashi entered the yeshiva in Mainz, it had existed for sixty-five years. Throughout those years, a general notebook was composed – the work of three generations of students – called the Kuntres Mainz. But whereas many of the other students adopted the notebook whole, Rashi sought to improve it. From his youth until his last day, he kept rewriting, erasing, and adding words to it. That perfectionism is the mark of supreme intellectual honesty that exhibits itself within his commentary.

Rashi's commentary to Chumash is a window not only to the understanding of the holy book of the Torah, but into Judaism in general, which is why its study is so necessary for old and young alike. Simply put, without Rashi it would be difficult for anyone to gain a proper insight into the value system of Judaism, its nuances and worldview. Rashi's commentary has withstood the vicissitudes of Jewish and general history and culture for almost a millennium. There is no equal to it in world scholarship and literature. It has the ability to bind generations together and to erase the sometimes artificial barriers of time and space, especially within a home and family.

Rashi's grandson, Rabbi Yaakov ben Meir (Rabenu Tam) stated, "I could perhaps have written a commentary to the Talmud the equal of Rashi's. But only Rashi, my holy grandfather, could have written such a commentary to Torah!"

It is no exaggeration to say that the Jewish people could not have sustained the exile without the Torah. The Torah gives us a connection to God, an understanding of where we come from, and a comprehension of why we are here now. It is also no exaggeration to say that, without Rashi, the Torah would have been forgotten.

Rashi modestly says over and over again, "I am only coming to tell you the simple meaning of the text"; yet in so doing, he preserved the Jewish people.

Through his latest installment, *The Family Rashi Book*, Rabbi Shalom Hammer can be credited with preserving the study of Rashi within the Jewish people. He presents a tool that can be utilized by Jewish educators and all Jewish families who wish to educate themselves and their children with an appreciation of the timeless words of this eternal teacher of Torah to Israel. This sefer is a marvelous addition to the Jewish home and, through its stimulating questions, it will enhance Torah knowledge and advance its study.

— *Rabbi Berel Wein*

ACKNOWLEDGMENTS

Baruch Hashem, this is the third *sefer* I have authored. One might think that writing becomes easier with each sefer and experience, but that is not the case. Every sefer is "a world of its own" that requires attention and consideration in order to see it to fruition.

I wish to acknowledge the following people who helped facilitate, each in their own way, the production of *The Family Rashi Book*.

This is the third time I have collaborated with Yaacov Peterseil and the first time I am working with Tzvi Mauer at Urim Publishing; it has proven to be a productive and pleasurable experience. I know it has been a challenging time for Yaacov and the new management and I wish them all good blessings and continued success.

Sara Rosenbaum edited this sefer with professionalism, and I am most impressed by her continual positive attitude throughout the demanding process.

Thank you to *Mori VeRabi*, Rabbi Berel Wein, who contributed to this sefer and is always a tremendous source of support and direction for me and my entire family.

I also want to acknowledge some of my dear friends and family who have been kind enough to financially facilitate the publication of this sefer.

The entire Tager *mishpacha* are very impressive people and close friends. These are passionate, sincere people who are interested in impacting the Jewish world in positive ways. Jonny, and Robbie and Trina, consistently help support my projects. I am very grateful and honored to be a part of their team.

It was a special privilege for me in my childhood to watch my cousin Adam evolve and develop into a sincerely religious Jew, and it has been particularly inspirational to witness how he – together with his lovely wife, Shani, and their beautiful children – fortified the foundations of a *Bayit Ne'eman Beyisrael*. Their contribution to this sefer demonstrates their commitment to spreading the words of Torah.

I grew up together with a *chevra* of "bandits" who had outstanding and outlandish personalities. One of my dearest friends from this chevra is Michael Ratzker. Michael and I went through primary, high school and college together (many claim that it is miraculous we made it that far). Even at a young age, Michael's outstanding attributes of warm friendliness and sincere *mentschlechkeit* were blatantly obvious and evidenced by his popularity. It is my privilege to be a *"ben bayit"* by the Ratzker family when I am in New Jersey, and I thank Michael and Drorit for their gracious hospitality.

Another old friend from high school days is Marc Hanzel. I was extremely moved as Marc agreed to help support this project without a moment's hesitation. I appreciate Marc and Cindy's gracious hospitality when I pass through the Philadelphia area.

I am impressed with Dr. and Mrs. Warren Sobol's readiness to assist in worthy causes, but most impressed by the modest and unassuming manner in which they do so. Warren and Maureen ask nothing more than to serve Hashem and instill in their children the passion with which to further their Jewish allegiance.

I have a number of dear friends from various countries whose contributions helped to assure that this work would be published and the words of Torah would proliferate:

Andrew and Veronique Berman, London, United Kingdom
Saun and Yve Borstock, Capetown, South Africa
Scott and Karen Evans, Miami, Florida
Dr. Jack and Rachel Greenspan, Columbus, Ohio
Jeff and Sara Mor, Bet Shemesh, Israel
Jonathan and Bracha Stefansky, Bet Shemesh, Israel

I wish them well and may the learning accomplished through their support of this sefer merit them and their families with *bracha vesimcha*.

Even during the challenging economic climate that we are experiencing, those mentioned above subscribe to *"harbatzat Torah"* and appreciate the importance of publishing this sefer that will, I'yH, promote Torah study and encourage an appreciation of *Rashi's* commentary.

This sefer is dedicated to my parents, Dr. David and Florence Hammer, who have guided me, my wife Gabi, and our six children with their love and wisdom. *Al tikrei banayich ela bonayich*. This sefer serves as only one of the many testaments to what they have built and accomplished in a life dedicated to *shmira bezehirut veavoda bezrizut*. May Hashem grant them strength and continued happiness.

To my beloved wife, Gabi, and our dear children, Bracha, Adena, Yaakov, Chamshush, Gila, and Srulie Boy, may all of our aspirations and desires reveal themselves through what is described in the pages of this sefer.

ילכו מחיל אל חיל יראה אל אלהים בציון

INTRODUCTION

The Talmud says:

> Rabbi Huna son of Rabbi Yehuda says in the name of Rabbi Ami, "One should always complete his recital of the weekly Torah portion together with the congregation by completing two readings of the weekly Torah portion and one reading of the Targum [Onkelas]…for one who completes the Torah portions with the greater congregation is privileged to longer days and longer years."

The *Shulchan Aruch HaRav* comments on the Talmud, that it is even greater to read Rashi's commentary on the Parsha than the Targum, because Rashi is based on the Talmud and explains more. *The Family Rashi Book* was written to help people fulfill this particular Mitzvah and encourage people to review Rashi's commentary on the weekly Parsha.

The first *sefer* I authored, *The Family Parsha Book*, was written to facilitate a familial review of the weekly Parsha around the Shabbat table. I received much positive feedback from people who thanked me for providing a learning tool that was both conducive to study and enjoyable at the same time. While *The Family Parsha Book* includes certain questions on Rashi within each Parsha, it does not offer an extensive review nor does it concentrate exclusively on Rashi's commentary on the Parsha. Therefore I decided to write a sefer that would focus on and help promote studying Rashi.

The Family Rashi Book follows the similar and successful format of *The Family Parsha Book*; it is a series of questions whose answers are arranged in an *Aleph-Bet* sequence whereby, in general, the first answer begins with an *aleph*, the second answer with a *bet*, etc. This sequence should encourage people to probe the *passuk* and Rashi for the correct answer to the question.

There are a number of guidelines to bear in mind while using the sefer. Firstly, if a question contains two letters – for example, aleph and bet – the answers are not always in proper sequence, so the first answer may start with a bet and the second answer with an aleph. In addition, the user should bear in mind that Rashi is a commentary on the words of the Torah and one must appreciate Rashi's derivation from the text of the passuk as well. Therefore, at times the question might be based on Rashi's commentary and the answer is found in the words of the passuk upon which Rashi based his comments.

To use *The Family Rashi Book* properly, one should have a *Chumash* and Rashi in hand, as every question is followed by the location of the passuk where its answer can be looked up. Most importantly, while the letters provide helpful hints, after finding the passuk, one should look for the answer within Rashi and not only for the letter in the alphabet. The goal is to understand what Rashi is telling us, and not only to find the letter that provides the answer. After finding the letter and the answer, it is essential to explain what Rashi means and how he arrived at his interpretation.

Some Family Parsha Book users might find that reviewing the Rashis within the Parsha is challenging, particularly around the time frame of the Shabbat meal, which is why it is important that this sefer be used other times as well over the course of Shabbat, or even during the week, by formally or informally reviewing the questions systematically (using the sefer as a guide).

Remember that many Rashis are covered within each Parsha but not all of them. For one to fulfill the Mitzvah described above, one must review all the Rashis on the Parsha. I have tried to offer a wide array of questions to keep things interesting and I concentrated for the most part on the key Rashis of each Parsha that would help the user appreciate the message(s) of the Parsha as well.

I sincerely hope this sefer encourages its readers to study commentary on the Torah and furthers the study of Rashi.

בראשית

Bereishit

Questions

א, ב The תורה begins with the word _____ so that in case the _____ claim that the Jewish people are thieves for conquering the land of the seven nations, בני ישראל can respond that all of the _____ belongs to הקדוש ברוך הוא, and since He created it, He can give it to a nation or take it away from them as He pleases. (1:1)

ג Anything that is not _____ from the land is called a שרץ. (1:20)

ד What are תנינים? (1:21)

ה In order to show that the world was created on the condition that בני ישראל accept the Torah, _____ at the conclusion of the sixth day of Creation. What are the two reasons why? (1:31)

ו This word teaches us that אדם and חוה heard the voice of 'ה walking in גן עדן. (3:8)

ז Why does the Torah say that Chava was created to be a "helper corresponding against" Adam? Can חוה be both a "helper" and "against" him at the same time? (2:20)

ח 'ה cut _____'s life short even though he was a צדיק, because 'ה was afraid that if he stayed alive, he would go astray. (5:24)

ט What was 'ה's plan for the fruit-bearing trees when He initially created them? (1:11)

י Why was למך's son called נח? (5:29)

כ We see that אדם was _____ because he blamed חוה for giving him to eat from the tree of knowledge. (3:12)

ל What was made smaller because it complained that two creations cannot share the same crown? (1:16)

מ From the words "ברא אלהים," we learn that at first, 'ה planned on creating the world with _____, but then, He decided to create the world based on _____. Why? (1:1)

נ After קין was punished, he went to live in the land of
_____, which received its name because it is a place where all
exiles _____. (4:16)

ס _____ means the counting of the generations since the creation
of man; it is referred to in the פסוק as _____. (5:1)

ע What is one thing we learn from the fact that 'ה said to the angels, "Let
us make Man in our image," and how do we learn this? (1:26)

פ _____ is a blessing from 'ה, which stems from the word
_____ and means to be fruitful and multiply. (1:22)

צ What did 'ה do with the dirt on the ground during the creation of
Man? (2:7)

ק _____ built a city, which he named after his son, חנוך. (4:17)

ר What did 'ה remove from the snake as a curse, in order to punish the
snake? (3:14)

ש Where does the word שמים come from? (Name at least two of three
answers.) (1:8)

ת The water that covered the land was called _____. (1:2)

Answers

א, ב. בראשית, אומות העולם, ארץ

Bereishit, Nations of the world, Land

ג. גבוה

Higher up

ד. דגים גדולים שבים

Large fish in the sea

ה. ה׳ הוסיף ה

Hashem added a [letter] hay.

One reason is because the letter ה has the numerical value of five, correspond-ing to the five books of the Torah. Hashem created all creations on condition that Bnei Yisrael would accept upon themselves the entire Torah. The second reason is because Hashem suspended all Creation until "the" sixth day (השישי) which cor-responds to "the" featured sixth day of סיון when the Torah was given.

ו. וישמעו

They heard

ז. זכה עזר לא זכה כנגדו להלחם

If one is worthy then [his mate] is helpful, if one is not worthy then [his mate] becomes his adversary.

ח. חנוך

Hanoch

ט. טעם העץ כטעם הפרי

The taste of the tree would be like the taste of the fruit on the tree.

י. ינח ממנו את עצבון ידינו

He will comfort us from toiling with our hands [by introducing the plow with which to work the land].

כ. כפר בטובה

He was ungrateful

ל. לבנה

The moon

מ. מדת הדין, מדת רחמים

The attribute of Judgment, The attribute of Mercy

   He saw that the world would not last if it were created based on the attribute of judgment, so He decided to base the creation of the world on the attribute of mercy.

נ. נוד, נדים שם

[the land of] wandering, wander there

ס. ספירת תולדות האדם, ספר תולדות האדם

counting the descendants of Adam, the book [account] of the descendants of Adam

ע. ענותנותו

[Hashem's] humility

   Hashem is solely responsible for making Man; however, in order to make the angels feel good and appease their jealousy of Man, He invited the angels to join Him, revealing His modesty.

פ. פרו ורבו, פרי

[The Mitzvah] to be fruitful and multiply, fruit

צ. צבר עפרו מכל האדמה מארבע רוחות

[Hashem] collected earth from all the land, from all four directions

ק. קין

Cain

ר. רגלים

[its] legs

ש. שא מים, שם מים, אש ומים שערבן זה בזה ועשה מהם שמים

"carry water," "water is there," a combination of fire and water, which [Hashem] mixed together and created the Heavens

ת. תהום

The deep

Questions

א The תורה says _____, which demonstrates that נח needed the support and assistance of Hashem, unlike _____, who was able to walk before Hashem. How does Rashi describe this second case? (6:9)

ב Which words in the תורה demonstrate the prohibition against eating a limb which was detached from a living animal? (9:4)

ג The world was filled with חמס, which means _____. (6:11)

ד The only living organisms that did not perish from the flood were the _____. (7:22)

ה Which word is read differently from the way it is written and why? (8:17)

ו Which word in the פרשה should have been written in plural form but is written in singular form and why? (9:23)

ז What does the תורה refer to when it says "ויעש נח" (Noach did)? (6:22)

ח Which kinds of creatures are also referred to as "ציפור כל כנף" (every bird of any kind of wing)? (7:14)

ח, ט The תורה says _____, which means that the ground dried up and became like _____. (8:13)

י What does a baby receive as it exits its mother's womb? (8:21)

כ What type of negative behavior did the people who built the tower demonstrate, much like their predecessor אדם? (11:5)

ל Prior to the sin of building the tower, the whole world spoke _____. (11:1)

מ Which words teach us that נח was lacking in his faith in ה' and how? (7:7)

נ The word דורות is _____ to demonstrate that there are some generations that do not need a sign of covenant with ה׳ because of the righteous people found in that generation. (9:12)

ס How does the תורה classically refer to the boundary of a land? (10:19)

ע "The earth had become corrupt" means that the earth was filled with _____ and _____. (6:11)

פ One of the descendants of יפת was תירס, who became the nation of _____. (10:2)

צ, ק Which two מצוות were given to שם and יפת, respectively, as a reward for preserving their father's dignity? (9:23)

ר What causes ה׳'s attribute of Mercy to turn into the attribute of Judgment? (8:1)

ש Even _____ were brought onto the Ark. (6:19)

ת What kind of "רוח" (spirit) did ה׳ cause to pass over the earth? (8:1)

Answers

א. את האלהים התהלך נח, אברהם, אברהם היה מתחזק ומהלך בצדקו מאליו
Noach walked with God, Avraham, Avraham would strengthen himself and walk on the path of righteousness on his own.

ב. בשר בנפשו דמו לא תאכלו
Flesh which is still with its soul, its blood you shall not eat.

ג. גזל
Thievery

ד. דגים שבים
Fish that were in the sea

ה. הוצא כתיב היצא קרי
The word is written הוצא (that they take out), but it is read היצא (should go out).
   The word Hayetze informs us that Noach should tell all the animals that they have to leave the ark, and the word Hotze informs us that if the animals would not leave after being told by Noach to do so, then he should force them out of the ark.

ו. ויקח
He took
   This demonstrates that although both Shem and Yephet were involved in preserving their father's dignity, Shem worked harder then Yephet to do so.

ז. זה בנין התיבה
This refers to construction of the Ark.

ח. חגבים
Grasshoppers

ח, ט. חרבו המים, טיט
The waters dried up, mud

י. יצר הרע
Evil Inclination

כ. כפו בטובה

Denied good [ungrateful]

ל. לשון הקודש

The holy language

מ. מפני מי המבול

Because of the waters of the flood

The Torah says that Noach and his family entered the ark because of the waters of the flood. Had the waters not forced them to, they may still have avoided entering the Ark altogether, which demonstrates a lack of trust in what Hashem had said would happen.

נ. נכתב חסר

written incomplete

ס. סוף ארצו

The end of his land [boundary]

ע. ערוה, עבודה זרה

Promiscuity, Idolatry

פ. פרס

Persia

צ, ק. ציצית, קבורת המת

Tzizit, Burying the dead

ר. רשעתן של רשעים

Wickedness of the Wicked

ש. שדים

Demons

ת. תנחומין

Comfort

לֶךְ לְךָ

Questions

א What do we learn from the fact that 'ה said to אברם, "To your descendants I have given this Land"? (15:18)

ב What did אברם mean when he told his nephew, לוט, "…if you go left, then I will go right, and if you go right, then I will go left"? (13:9)

ג, ד The Euphrates river is called "_____" because it is _____ to ארץ ישראל. (15:18)

ה, ו The Torah reveals that שרה _____ toward her maidservant, _____, from the words, "_____." (16:6)

ז אברם asked 'ה in what _____ would his children be eternal, and 'ה answered, "In the _____ of the sacrifices." (15:6)

ח The word _____ refers to אליעזר. This word is related to _____, which means to educate, and _____, which means to dedicate. (14:14)

ט The תורה says that אברם was "כבד מאוד במקנה" (heavily laden with livestock). This means that his livestock were _____. (13:2)

י After 'ה told אברהם that he would have a son, אברהם laughed and said to himself, "Would someone one hundred years old have a child?" What do we learn from this reaction? (17:17)

כ A Jew who lives outside of ארץ ישראל is _____. (17:8)

ל When 'ה instructed אברם, "_____," He emphasized to אברם that it would be _____ and _____. (12:1)

מ What would אברם receive a lot of in the form of one of the ברכות from 'ה? (12:1)

נ Which word demonstrates that whenever 'ה says something, it is considered done? (15:18)

ס לוט pitched his tent and set up his camp right by _____ even though the people of _____ were wicked. (13:12,13)

ע, פ The _____ who came to tell אברם about the war between the kings was _____, according to _____ of the מדרש. _____ was called a _____ because he _____. (14:13)

צ What kind of value do we see that אברם and שרה had in their marriage based on אברם's words to שרה, "Now, I have known that you appear to be a beautiful woman," and how do these words demonstrate this value? (12:11)

ק What did אברם mean when he told לוט, "We are men and brothers"? (13:8)

ר The "voice of שרי" refers to the _____. (16:2)

ש The meaning of ה''s name, _____, is _____. (17:1)

ת One of the blessings ה' gave אברם at the ברית בין הבתרים was _____, which means that ישמעאל would do _____ in his lifetime and that עשו would not pursue _____ while אברם was alive. (15:15)

Answers

א. אמירתו של הקדוש ברוך הוא כאלו היא עשויה

The statements of Hakadosh Baruch Hu are as good as done.

ב. בכל אשר תשב לא אתרחק ממך ואעמוד לך למגן ולעזר

No matter where you settle I [Hashem] will not be far from you and I will serve as your protector and helper.

ג, ד. גדול, דבוק

Great, Connected to

ה, ו. היתה משעבדת בה בקושי, הגר, ותענה שרי

She would enforce upon her hard labor, Hagar, Sarai afflicted [her]

ז. זכות, זכות

merit, merit

ח. חניכיו, חנוך לנער, חנוכת המזבח

his students, educate the youth, dedication of the Altar

ט. טעון משאות

[the animals] were loaded heavily with supplies

י. יש תמיהות שהן קימות

There are questions of astonishment that are legitimate.

כ. כמי שאין לו אלוה

Likened to someone who has no God

ל. לך לך, להנאתך, לטובתך

Go for yourself, for your own benefit, for your own good

מ. ממון

money

נ. נתתי

I have given

ס. סדום, סדום

Sdom, Sdom

ע, פ. פליט, עוג , פשוטו, עוג, פליט, פלט מן המלחמה

fugitive, Og, simple context, Og, fugitive, fled from the war

צ. צניעות

modesty

The verse says, "Now I have known about your beauty," which, according to the Midrash, implies that up until now, Avram was not aware of Sara's beauty because of the modest existence between them.

ק. קרובים

relatives

ר. רוח הקודש שבה

The Holy Spirit within her

ש. שדי, שיש די באלהותי לכל בריה

Shadai, there is enough of My Divinity for every creation

ת. תקבר בשיבה טובה, תשובה, תרבות רעה

"You shall be buried in good old age," repentance, wicked conduct

Questions

א   Why did ה' send אברהם three angels to visit him; why not just send one? (18:2)

ב   The תורה says that ה' "remembered" שרה – in what way was this fulfilled? (21:1)

ג   When יצחק grew older, אברהם made a משתה that was _____, which means that he invited the _____. (21:8)

ד   Before ה' decided to destroy סדום, He descended to see them. This teaches _____ that they should not judge in _____ until they see clearly what happened. (18:21)

ה   What did ה' do for אברהם to ensure that he would not be bothered by guests while still in pain from his ברית מילה? What did ה' do for אברהם when He saw that אברהם was upset that he did not have any guests to entertain? (18:1)

ו   _____ is another word for _____, which means that they hastened. (19:15)

ז   Who is the נער? (18:7)

ח   אברהם appeals to ה' not to kill סדום by saying _____, which means _____. (18:25)

ט   אברהם ran to prepare the three tongues of three bulls, which were both tender and _____. (18:7)

י   Where is ארץ המוריה? (22:2)

ב, ל, מ   The expression _____ is a _____ and refers to Avraham's instructing his children to keep the way of Hashem. (18:19) The word _____ is a _____. (21:9)

נ   אברהם awoke early to prepare for עקידת יצחק, which showed that he was _____. (22:3)

ס, ע אברהם took a _____ for the עקידה that was called a מאכלת. Why was it called this? (22:6)

פ These words reveal why לוט did not want to leave סדום. Explain. (19:19)

צ What do we learn about שרה from the fact that the angels asked אברהם, "Where is your wife, Sara?" (18:9)

ק The site of the עקידה was referred to by אברהם as "ה' יראה," which means that it was a place where he would offer _____. (22:14)

ר What kind of behavior did ישמעאל follow, causing אברהם to get upset? (21:11)

ש What do we learn from the fact that the angels pretended to eat the food that אברהם gave them, even though angels do not normally eat? (18:8)

ת סדום was turned into a _____. (19:28)

Answers

א. אחד לבשר את שרה, אחד להפוך את סדום, אחד לרפאות את אברהם; אין מלאך אחד עושה שתי שליחיות

One to bring tidings to Sara, one to overturn Sodom, one to heal Avraham; One angel does not perform two missions.

ב. בהריון

[with] pregnancy

ג. גדול, גדולי הדור

grand, great [leaders] of the generation

ד. דיינים, דיני נפשות

Judges, laws pertaining to corporal punishment

ה. הוציא הקדוש ברוך הוא חמה מנרתיקה, הביא המלאכים עליו

[Hashem] brought the sun out of its sheath, He brought the angels to him

ו. ויאצו, ודחיקו

Both mean they hastened

ז. זה ישמעאל

This is Ishmael

ח. חללה לך, חולין הוא לך

It would be sacrilege to you, it is profane for you

ט. טוב

good

י. ירושלים

Jerusalem

כ, ל, מ. כי ידעתיו, לשון חיבה, מצחק, לשון עבודה זרה

For I have cherished him, an expression of endearment, mocking, an expression of idolatry

נ. נזדרז למצוה

He moved promptly to perform the commandment

ס, ע. סכין, על שם שאוכלת את הבשר

A knife, because it "eats" the flesh [that it cuts]

פ. פן תדבקני הרעה

Lest the evil attach itself to me
Lot realized that when he was amongst the people of Sdom, he was a righteous
person in comparison to them. If he would leave Sdom and be amongst righteous
people, then his wickedness, in comparison, would be revealed.

צ. צנוע היתה

[that] she was modest

ק. קרבנות

sacrificial offerings

ר. רעה

evil behavior

ש. שלא ישנה אדם מן המנהג

That a person should not deviate from the custom [of the place he is in.]

ת. תמור של עשן

A pillar of smoke

Questions

א Where was אברהם's birthplace? (24:7)

ב When Hashem blessed אברהם _____, it meant he would have a _____. (24:1)

ג Even אברהם's _____ were careful of _____, as they were muzzled so that they would not eat from fields that did not belong to their master. (24:10)

ד What concept do we learn from the words "וינחם יצחק אחרי אמו"? How? (24:67)

ה אברהם married קטורה who was _____. (25:1)

ו The word _____ is of the verb form _____, which is similar to _____ and _____. (24:65)

ז One reason מערת המכפילה was given its name was because there were many _____ buried there. (23:9)

ח What do we learn that שרה never did, from the fact that the תורה delineates the years of her life? (23:1)

ט, י, כ When שרה was _____ years old, she had the _____ of a seven-year-old, and all of שרה's years were connected by her _____. (23:1)

ל Why does the תורה delineate the years that ישמעאל lived? Explain. (25:17)

מ, נ, ס Someone who is _____ has to hold in his hand something used for a _____, such as a _____. (24:2)

ע What happened to the water in the well when רבקה approached it? (24:17)

פ In order to ensure that his camels would not graze from private fields, אליעזר would tie _____ shut. (24:32)

צ Regarding what kind of people does the תורה say "ויאסף אל עמיו"? (25:17)

ק This city received its name either because of the four giants who were there or because of the four great couples who were buried there. (23:2)

ר When אברהם says to the בני חת, "...אם יש את נפשיכם," the word "נפשיכם" means _____. (23:8)

ש אליעזר left אברהם's house with "כל טוב אדוניו בידו," which refers to a _____ in which אברהם gave all his possessions to יצחק. (24:10)

ש, ת ישמעאל did _____ before אברהם died and this was the _____ referring to אברהם. (25:9)

Answers

א. אור כשדים

Ur Kasdim

ב. בכל, בן

with everything, son

ג. גמלים, גזילה

camels, stealing

ד. דרך ארץ

The way of the world (normal patterns of behavior)
Normally a person clings to his mother for comfort, but when she dies, he then turns to his wife for comfort. This is demonstrated as the verse says first that Rivka became Yitzchak's wife and immediately after, that he was consoled after his mother's death.

ה. הגר

Hagar

ו. ותתכס, ותתפעל, ותקבר, ותשבר

she covered herself, third person feminine reflexive verb form, she was buried, she was broken

ז. זוגות

couples

ח. חטאים

Sins

ט, י, כ. כ׳, יופי, טובה

twenty, beauty, goodness

ל. ליחס בהן שנותיו של יעקב

To trace the years of Yakov
By delineating the years of Yishmael, the Torah reveals that Yishmael hosted Yakov for fourteen years prior to his arrival in Lavan's house.

מ, נ, ס. נשבע, מצוה, ספר תורה

swore, mitzvah, Torah

ע. עלו המים לקראתה

The water rose up toward her

פ. פיהם

their mouths

צ. צדיקים

Righteous people

ק. קרית ארבע

Kiryat Arba

ר. רצונכם

your [plural] desire

ש. שטר מתנה

Document for a gift

ש, ת. תשובה, שיבה טובה

repentance, good old age

Questions

א What did עשו mean when he requested "הלעיטני נא מן האדם האדם הזה" from יעקב, and which הלכה can we learn from עשו's request? (25:30)

ב יצחק told עשו that יעקב took his ברכה _____, which means _____. (27:35)

ג What do we learn from רבקה's statement "אם כן למה זה אנוכי"? (25:22)

ד אברהם was praised for listening to the מצות of ה'. What do these מצות refer to? Cite examples. (26:5)

ה What was יעקב doing to עשו as he exited his mother's womb? (25:26)

ו In יעקב's bracha, _____ means not only יתן, but _____. (27:28)

ז Who does the "אחד העם" refer to? (26:10)

ח When יצחק contemplated going down to Egypt, ה' told him that he does not belong in _____. (26:2)

ט יצחק instructed עשו to bring him deer meat and רבקה in turn told יעקב to bring יצחק goat's meat because _____. (27:9)

י Who does the תורה refer to as תולדות יצחק בן אברהם? (25:19)

כ When would רבקה feel extra kicking in her womb during her pregnancy? (25:22)

ל יעקב hid in the house of עבר on his way _____ in order _____ from him. (28:9)

מ יעקב fled from עשו and went to learn תורה but during that time, he did not see his father, יצחק, for twenty-two years and he could not fulfill the מצוה of כיבוד אב ואם. Therefore he was punished and he, consequently, did not see his son, יוסף, for twenty-two years. This represents _____. (28:9)

נ, ס יצחק instructed עשו to sharpen his _____, to ensure that he would not eat _____. (27:3)

ע, פ The reason why יעקב gave עשו _____ to eat is because it was the day that אברהם died; one eats these _____ as a sign of mourning because, just like an _____ does not have a _____, so, too, a mourner does not open his _____ out of sadness. (25:30)

צ יצחק's תפילות were more effective then רבקה's because the תפילה of a _____ ben _____ is greater then the תפילה of a _____. (25:21)

ק יעקב's _____ was gentle and used gentle tones, as he said to his father, יצחק, "_____." עשו ordered his father Yitzchak to stand, an example of _____, which means he was demanding. (27:22)

ר Where was נחל גרר? (26:17)

ש At what age do people start taking notice of your deeds? (25:27)

ת What kind of life can צדיקים expect to lead? (27:29)

Answers

א. אפתח פי ושפוך הרבה לתוכה, אין אובסין את הגמל בשבת אבל מלעיטין אותו

I will open my mouth and pour a lot into it, One is forbidden from stuffing a camel on Shabbat but one is permitted to pour food into its mouth.

ב. במרמה, בחכמה

with cleverness, with wisdom

ג. גדול צער העיבור

Great is the pain of pregnancy

ד. דברים שאילו לא נכתבו ראויין הם להצטוות כגון גזל ושפיכות דמים

Matters which, had they not been written, would still have been expected commandments such as thievery and murder

ה. היה אוחז בו לעכבו

He was holding on to obstruct him [from exiting the womb].

ו. ויתן לך, ויחזור ויתן

God will give you, He will give and give again

ז. זה המלך

This [refers to] the King.

ח. חוץ לארץ

land outside of Israel

ט. טעם הגדי כטעם הצבי

the taste of goat meat is like the taste of deer meat

י. יעקב ועשו האמורים בפרשה

Yakov and Esav who are mentioned in the Parsha.

כ. כשהיתה עוברת על פתחי תורה של שם ועבר יעקב רץ ומפרכס לצאת עוברת על פתחי עבודה זרה עשו מפרכס לצאת

When she would pass by the entrance of the institution of תורה*study of* שם *and* עבר*then* יעקב *would kick and toss and when she passed by the entrance to a house of idol worship then* עשו *would kick to exit her womb.*

ל. לבית לבן, ללמוד תורה

To Lavan's house, to study Torah

מ. מדה כנגד מדה

Measure for measure

נ, ס. סכין, נבלות

knife, carcasses which have not been slaughtered

ע, פ. עדשים, עדשים, עדש, פה, פה

lentils, lentils, lentil, mouth, mouth

צ. צדיק בן צדיק, צדיק בן רשע

righteous person who is the child of a righteous person, righteous person who is the child of a wicked person

ק. קול, קום נא, קנטוריא דבר

voice, get up please, antagonistic speech

ר. רחוק מן העיר

Far from the city

ש. שלש עשרה

Thirteen years old

ת. תחלתם יסורים וסופן שלוה

Their beginning is marked by suffering and their end is marked by tranquility.

Questions

א, ב   The _____ of יעקב are referred to as his _____. (31:46)

ג   יעקב assured לבן that he was not involved in _____ or _____. (31:39)

ד   This word means to chase after. (31:36)

ה   What does a צדיק mean to a city? (28:10)

ו   Another word for תפילה. (28:11)

ז   יעקב placed the _____ before the women out of respect, but עשו placed the women before the _____. (31:17)

ח   Someone who does not have children is _____. (30:1)

ט   יעקב instructed לבן to remove every sheep that was _____. These are sheep that have _____, meaning wide, large patches on them. (30:32)

י   What do we learn from the fact that the תורה says "ויצא יעקב" as opposed to just writing where he was headed – "וילך חרנה"? (28:10)

כ   In what manner did יעקב lift the stone from the well? (29:10)

ל   Why did יעקב clearly need ה's promise that He would guard him at this point? (28:15)

מ, נ   יעקב _____ לבן because he thought maybe יעקב was hiding _____ in his mouth. (29:13)

ס   יעקב gave _____ to רחל so that he could recognize her and marry her. רחל in turn gave the _____ to לאה so she wouldn't be embarrassed because she was marrying יעקב first. (29:25)

ע   Name one of the four types of people who are considered dead, even while alive. (29:11)

פ, צ   The תואר of a person refers to the _____. (29:17)

ק What did ה׳ do to ארץ ישראל after יעקב laid down to rest? (28:13)

ר What would the flocks of sheep do by the well? (29:3)

ש Another expression referring to a מקום תפילה. (28:17)

ת _____ are male goats. (30:35)

Answers

א, ב. בנים, אחים

children, brothers

ג. גנובת יום, גנובת לילה

stealing by day, stealing by night

ד. דלקת

You have chased

ה. הוא הודה הוא זיוה הוא הדרה

He is its majesty, he is its beauty, he is its glory.

ו. ויפגע

Encountered

ז. זכרים, זכרים

males

ח. חשוב כמת

considered as if he is dead

ט. טלוא, טלאי

spotted, patches

י. יציאת צדיק מן המקום עושה רושם

When a righteous person leaves a place, it leaves an impression.

כ. כאדם שמעביר את הפקק מעל פי צלוחית

Like a person who removes a stopper from a flask

ל. לפי שהיה ירא מעשו ולבן

Because he was afraid of עשו and לבן.

מ, נ. נשק, מרגליות

kissed, precious stones

ס. סימנים, סימנים

signs

ע. עני

Poor person

פ, צ. צורת פרצוף

shape of the face

ק. קיפל הקדוש ברוך הוא כל ארץ ישראל תחתיו
הקדוש ברוך הוא *folded up all of* ארץ ישראל *and placed it under him.*

ר. רגילים היו להאסף לפי שהיתה האבן גדולה
They would regularly gather there because the stone was large.

ש. שער השמים

Gates of heaven

ת. תישים

male goats

Questions

א Which concept do we learn based on the way יעקב placed his family, with the handmaids and their children first, followed by לאה and רחל and their children, in preparation for his meeting with עשו? (33:2)

ב דינה was referred to as _____ and not _____. Why? (34:1)

ג The wording _____ demonstrates that ה׳ blessed יעקב that his children would multiply as many in numbers as the _____ of the world. (35:11)

ד Why did יעקב tell עשו that he had a "שור וחמור" when he actually owned quite a few? (32:6)

ה What do the Rabbis say regarding the relationship between עשו and יעקב? (33:4)

ו What were the two emotional reactions that יעקב experienced when the messengers informed him that עשו was approaching with four hundred men and why? (32:8)

ז ה׳ promised יעקב that his _____ would be both like the sand of the sea and the dust of the land. (32:13)

ח יעקב resided in סכת for eighteen _____ and during the _____, he lived in a house. (33:17)

ט שמעון and לוי instruct the city of שכם to make themselves _____, which means to destroy their עבודה זרה . (35:2)

י _____ knew that his mother was _____ so he stood in front of her blocking her from עשו because perhaps _____. (33:7)

כ The prohibition of eating from the גיד הנשה includes the _____, which refers to _____. (32:33)

ל Why were שמעון and לוי called אחי דינה? (34:25)

מ Who did יעקב send toward the land of אדום? (32:4)

נ שמעון and לוי informed שכם that they would be _____ and _____ only when שכם would be _____ . (34:15)

ס What type of tree is the אלה? (35:4)

ע Who are "the men" whom יעקב "struggled with and overcame"? (32:29)

פ What did יעקב forget by the stream? (32:25)

צ יעקב was _____ as the sun rose. (32:32)

ק יעקב purchased land from חמור with a small coin called a _____
(33:19).

ר Whom does the אלופי בני עשו refer to? (36:15)

ש When יעקב arrived to _____ , he was: (a) _____ , which
means _____ ; (b) _____ , which means _____ ; and
(c) _____ , which means _____ . (33:18)

ת Who chose to be a concubine in עשו's family in order to be related to
אברהם אבינו? (36:12)

Answers

א. אחרון אחרון חביב

The most endeared is placed last in line

ב. בת לאה, בת יעקב

the daughter of Leah, the daughter of Yakov
Because she would often go outside as did her mother, Leah.

ג. גוי וקהל גוים, גוים

a nation and an assembly of nations, nations

ד. דרך ארץ לומר על שוורים הרבה שור

It is the accepted way of the world for one to refer to many oxen as "ox".

ה. הלכה היא בידוע שעשו שונא ליעקב

It is a known rule that Esav hates Yakov.

ו. ויירא שמא יהרג, ויצר לו אם יהרג הוא את אחרים

He was frightened that perhaps he would be killed, He was distressed that perhaps he would have to kill others.

ז. זרע

seed (offspring)

ח. חודש, חורף

months, winter

ט. טהור

pure

י. יוסף, יפת תאר, יתלה בה עיניו אותו רשע

Yosef, of beautiful countenance, the wicked [Esav] will set his eyes upon her

כ. כף, כל בשר גבוה ותלול ועגול

ball [of the thighbone], any [part of the] meat that is raised and whose shape is rounded

ל. לפי שמסרו עצמן עליה

Because they risked [their lives] for her

מ. מלאכים ממש

Actual Angels

נ. נאות לכם, נתרצה לכם, נימול

pleasant to you, accepting of you, circumcised

ס. סרק

[A] non-fruit-bearing tree

ע. עשו ולבן

Esav and Lavan

פ. פכים קטנים

small flasks

צ. צולע

limping

ק. קשיטה

type of small coin

ר. ראשי משפחות

Heads of the families

ש. שכם, שלם בגופו, שנתרפא מצלעתו, שלם בממונו, שלא חסר כלום, שלם בתורתו, שלא שכח תלמודו בבית לבן

Shechem, his body was whole, heeled of his limp, financially intact, was not missing anything, completely wholesome in his Torah learning, during the time he lived in the house of Lavan he did not forget any Torah he had learned prior to his arrival

ת. תימנע

Timna

Questions

א יוסף told his father that his brothers _____. (37:2)

ב The תורה refers to יעקב's sons- and daughters-in-law as _____ and _____; from here we learn that a person does not refrain from calling his son-in-law _____ and daughter-in-law _____. (37:35)

ג Who was the איש who found יוסף wandering in the fields? (37:15)

ד Why did the brothers dip יוסף's coat specifically in goat's blood? (37:31)

ה, ו, ז יהודה instructed his son אונן to marry תמר _____ for the sake of establishing _____ and having sons because _____. (38:8)

ח What is a כתונת? (37:23)

ט The שר האופים saw that יוסף was _____ at interpreting the dreams. (40:5)

י What do the תולדות of יעקב refer to? (37:2)

כ Why couldn't יהודה see or recognize who תמר was? (38:15)

ל Why did יעקב scold יוסף after he told him about the dreams he had? (37:10)

מ The תורה says that יוסף was a נער, which means that he was involved in _____, as he would _____ and _____. (37:2)

נ What do we learn from the fact that תמר would not embarrass יהודה in public and prove him wrong? (38:25)

ס After יוסף would _____ his dream to his brothers, he would then go and _____ to his father again in front of them. (37:10)

ע An _____ refers to someone who is from _____ and from the children of _____. (39:14)

פ What kind of events happen in שכם? (37:14)

צ The twins that תמר would give birth to were to be _____. (38:27)

ק Name one of the characteristics of the type of baskets the Baker had. (40:16)

ר The Egyptians are called _____, which means arrogant. This is why one should not place his faith in them as Yosef did with the שר המשקים. (40:23)

ש The תורה says "ה' אתו" regarding יוסף. What does this mean? (39:3)

ת A person is able to receive _____ for someone who has died, but one cannot receive _____ for someone who is still alive. (37:35)

Answers

א. אכלו אבר מן החי

ate limbs detached from a live animal

ב. בניו, בנותיו, בנו, בתו

his sons, his daughters ,his son, his daughter

ג. גבריאל

Gavriel

ד. דמו דומה לשל אדם

Its blood is similar to human's blood

ה, ו, ז. ויבם אותה, זרע, הבן יקרא על שם המת

Relate to her as wife of your deceased brother, offspring (lit. "seed"), the son is named after the deceased

ח. חלוק

A cloak

ט. טוב

good

י. ישוביהם וגלגוליהם

Where they settled and where they traveled

כ. כי כסתה פניה

Because she covered up her face

ל. לפי שהיה מטיל שנאה עליו

Because he brought hatred upon himself

מ. מעשה נערות, מתקן בשערו, ממשמש בעיניו

performing actions associated with youth, set his hair, groom his eyes

נ. נוח לו לאדם שיפיל עצמו לכבשן האש ואל ילבין פני חברו ברבים

[That] it is preferable for one to cast himself into a fiery furnace then to embarrass his friend in public.

ס. ספר, ספרו

report, report to him

ע. עברי, עבר הנהר, עבר

Ivri [Hebrew], the other side of the [Euphrates] river, Ever

פ. פרענות

bad events

צ. צדיקים

righteous

ק. קלופים

stripped

ר. רהבים

arrogant

ש. שם שמים שגור בפיו

The name of Heaven [Hashem] is fluent in his mouth.

ת. תנחומין, תנחומין

comfort, comfort

מקץ

Questions

א, ב _____ because _____. This is demonstrated as the שר המשקים referred to יוסף _____. (41:12)

ב, ג A _____ is a place that was used as a _____ and constructed like a _____. (41:14)

ד Which word means that the cows in פרעה's dream were scrawny? (41:19)

ה יוסף rode in the _____ מרכבת, which is _____ because it was _____. (41:43)

ו With which words did יהודה promise יעקב that he would bring בנימין back to him alive? (43:9)

ז The brothers said to יוסף, "The money we found in the mouths of our sacks we returned to you from Canaan; how could we have stolen from our master silver and gold?" What kind of statement is this? (44:8)

ח When יוסף accused his brother of stealing, their response was, " _____," which means _____. (44:7)

ט Another word for bones. (41:8)

י _____ told his brothers to bring בנימין to him so that "_____," which means _____ and _____. (42:20)

כ, ל The words "_____" refer _____. (43:9)

מ, נ The word _____ means _____. (41:32)

ס, ע Merchants and merchandise are referred to as _____ and _____. Why? (42:34)

פ Where would people who traveled through Egypt normally stay? (43:18)

צ This word means the first meal of the day. (43:16)

ק _____ is a type of bowing where one lowers his _____, which is the head. (43:28)

ר How does the תורה classically describe something (such as the cows in פרעה's dream) that is scrawny and lacking meat? (41:19)

ש The שר המשקים described יוסף as a נער, which means a _____. (41:12)

ת Which food of the Egyptians' was spoiled by the famine? (41:55)

מקץ

Answers

א, ב. ארורים הרשעים, אין טובתם שלמה, בלשון בזיון
Cursed are the wicked, their goodness is not complete, degrading terms

ב, ג. בור, בית הסוהר, גומא
pit, prison, hole [in the ground]

ד. דלות
scrawny

ה. המשנה, השניה למרכבתו, המהלכת אצל שלו
Second, the second chariot, [chariot] which rides along next to [Pharaoh's]

ו. והצגתיו לפניך
[I will] stand him up before you

ז. זה אחד מעשרה קל וחומר האמורים בתורה
This is one of ten kal vechomers stated in the Torah.

ח. חלילה לעבדיך מעשות כדבר הזה, חולין הוא לנו
It is unseemly for your servants to do such a thing, it is profane for us

ט. טימי
bones [in Aramaic]

י. יוסף, יאמנו דבריכם, יתאמתו, יתקימו
Yosef, your words will be verified, come true, take place

כ, ל. כל הימים, לעולם הבא
all the days, the world to come

מ, נ. נכון, מזמן
correct, ready

ס, ע. סוחרים, סחורה, על שם שמחזרים וסובבים אחר הפרקמטיא
Merchants, merchandise, because they [merchants] pursue and chase after business

פ. פונדקאות

inns

צ. צהרים

afternoon [referring to the first meal of the day]

ק. קידה, קדקד

bowing, head

ר. רכות

scrawny

ש. שוטה

simpleton

ת. תבואתם שאצרו

their stored wheat

Questions

א When the תורה says that יעקב settled in _____, it is referring to _____. (47:27)

ב What does טפכם refer to? (47:24)

ג יוסף introduced פרעה to five of his brothers who had the least amount of _____ and who did not look like _____ because if פרעה thought that they were _____, he would make them his soldiers. (47:2)

ד Why did the brothers tell יוסף that they had not wanted to bring בנימין to Egypt? (44:22)

ה, ו From the words "_____," we learn that _____. (44:29)

ז Why did יוסף send wine to יעקב? (45:23)

ח The תורה refers to ה' as "אלהי אבי יצחק" and makes no reference to אברהם. What do we learn from this? (46:1)

ט How does the תורה refer to ארץ גושן? (45:18)

י, כ יהודה said to יוסף, "_____," which means _____. He also told יוסף, "_____," which means that יוסף was important to him _____. (44:18)

ל יוסף told his brothers, "_____," which means that ה' sent him, "_____." (45:5)

מ, נ What was the brothers' reaction after יוסף told them who he was, and why? (45:3)

ס, ע, פ יוסף sent יעקב _____, which were a _____ that he remembered that they had learned _____ together. (45:27)

צ The תורה says that יוסף cried on יעקב's _____ twice, which demonstrates that he cried a lot. (46:29)

ויגש

ק   What is another way of saying that the land of Egypt belonged to פרעה? (47:20)

ר   What was יעקב's reaction when he heard that יוסף was alive, and what does it mean? (45:28)

ש   What was יעקב reciting when he was first reunited with יוסף? (46:29)

ת   What did פרעה tell the brothers to load up their animals with? (45:17)

Answers

א. ארץ מצרים, ארץ גשן

land of Egypt, land of Goshen

ב. בנים קטנים

young children

ג. גבורה, גבורים, גבורים

strength, strong men, strong men

ד. דואגים אנו שמא ימות בדרך

"We are worried perhaps he will die en route [to Egypt]."

ה, ו. וקרהו אסון, השטן מקטרג בשעת סכנה

A tragic accident will happen to him, the Satan harms most during times of danger

ז. זקנים נוחה הימנו

[The minds of] the elderly are comforted by it.

ח. חייב אדם בכבוד אביו יותר מכבוד זקנו

One is obligated to honor one's father more then one's grandfather.

ט. טוב מצרים

The best part of Egypt

י, כ. ידבר נא עבדך, יכנסו דברי באזניך, כי כמוך כפרעה, כמלך

Please allow your servant to speak, my words should enter your ears, for you are likened to Pharaoh, like a king

ל. למחיה שלחני אלהים לפניכם, להיות לכם למחיה

God sent me ahead of you to help you live, to serve for you as a supporter of life

מ, נ. נבהלו מפניו, מפני הבושה

They were startled by him, because they were deeply embarrassed.

ס, ע, פ. עגלות, סימן, פרשת עגלה ערופה

wagons, sign, the passage regarding the calf whose neck is broken

צ. צואריו

neck

ק. קנויה לו

belongs to him

ר. רב לי שמחה וחדוה

I have much happiness and gladness

ש. שמע

The Shma prayer

ת. תבואה

wheat

ויחי

Questions

א When יעקב heard that יוסף was approaching his bedside, he strengthened himself, sat up, and said _____. (48:2)

ב What does the תורה say with regards to יוסף's beauty and what does this mean? (49:22)

ג, ד The blessing יעקב gave to יהודה, _____, refers to _____. (49:8)

ה, ו The תורה says, "_____," which means that יעקב _____. (47:31)

ז What kind of animal was בנימין compared to and what does this animal do? (49:27)

ח יעקב refers to his _____, which refers to his _____. (48:22)

ט What was the ברכה that משה gave to אשר demonstrating that his land was filled with olive trees? (49:20)

י One part of the ברכות given to דן was "_____ דן" – this means _____. (49:16)

כ יעקב blessed אפרים and מנשה that they should be _____. (48:16)

ל What did יעקב want to do when he assembled his sons around him? (49:1)

מ, נ יוסף's sons _____ are referred to as _____. (48:16)

ס, ע Why did יעקב insist that he did not want to be buried in מצרים? (47:29)

פ An expression of thought. (48:11)

צ Whose daughters are referred to in the ברכה given to יוסף (מנשה)? (49:22)

ק, ר When בני ישראל would be cast into גלות, _____ would come out from her _____ and cry and ask for mercy for her people as it says, "_____." (48:7)

ר יעקב bowed toward _____ because the Shechina rests above the _____ of the ill. (47:31)

ש Another word for snake. (49:17)

ת יששכר bent his shoulders to bear the burden of _____. (49:15)

Answers

א. אף על פי שהוא בני מלך הוא אחלק לו כבוד

Even though he is my son he is a king I will show him respect

ב. בנות צעדה עלי שור, בנות מצרים היו צועדות על החומה להסתכל ביופיו

Girls stepped up to gaze, the girls of Egypt would step on and scale the walls [of the city] to gaze upon his beauty.

ג. גדעון

Gideon

ג, ד. גור אריה, דוד

lion's cub, David

ה, ו. וישתחו ישראל על ראש המטה, הפך עצמו לצד השכינה

Yisrael prostrated on the head of the bed, he turned toward the side of the Divine Presence

ז. זאב הוא אשר יטרף

He is a wolf who will maul

ח. חרב, חכמה

sword, wisdom

ט. טבל בשמן רגלו

He will dip his feet in oil

י. ידין עמו, ינקם נקמת עמו מפלשתים

[Dan] will instill justice in his people, seek revenge upon the Philistines for his people.

כ. כדגים הללו שפרים ורבים ואין עין הרע שולטת בהם

Like fish that multiply and become numerous and the evil eye has no effect on them

ל. לגלות את הקץ

To reveal the end of days

מ, נ. מנשה ואפרים, נערים

Menashe and Ephrayim, young men

ס, ע. סופה ליהיות עפרה כנים

In the end its ground will be lice infested

פ. פללתי

thought

צ. צלפחד

Tzelaphchad

ק, ר. רחל, קבר, קול ברמה נשמע

Rachel, grave, a voice is heard from up high

ר. ראש המיטה, ראש

the head of the bed, head

ש. שפיפון

snake

ת. תורה

Torah

שמות
Shemot

Questions

א, ב   The _____ of פרעה told him that a _____ would be born who would save בני ישראל (1:16)

ג   ה' expected משה to return to מצרים and to be _____. (4:21)

ד   Why does the תורה describe משה's hand as מצרעת כשלג – leprous like snow? (4:6)

ה   Reference to the place where בני ישראל would receive the תורה, three months after יציאת מצרים. (3:12)

ו   Which words in the פסוק demonstrate that משה saw בני ישראל's suffering and grieved with them? (2:11)

ז   ה' instructed משה to gather _____ who were not _____ but rather _____ to go with him to face פרעה. (3:16)

ח   משה rode on a _____ on his way to מצרים as it was the same _____ that אברהם _____ for עקידת יצחק. (4:20)

ט   משה was placed in a wicker basket that was lined on the inside with _____ so that he was spared the unpleasant scent of pitch from the outside. (2:3)

י, כ   How many of the זקנים left משה and אהרן as they approached פרעה's palace and why? (5:1)

ל   Why were בני ישראל counted again at the beginning of שמות when they were already counted at the end of בראשית? (1:1)

מ   After ה' told משה to go to מצרים and take בני ישראל out, he replied, "_____," which means _____? (3:11)

נ   What happened to the house when משה was _____? (2:2)

ס   This word means swampland. (2:3)

ע   What does the Torah mean when it says that Pharaoh did not know who Yosef was? (1:8)

פ, צ One of the midwives' names was _____, which means
_____. (1:15)

ק When בת פרעה opened the basket she saw a נער בכה – a "young
man crying." Why was משה called a young man when he was only a
baby? (2:6)

ר משה's basket was lined with plaster because a צדיק should not have
to smell the _____ of the tar (on the outside of the basket). (2:3)

ש משה was instructed by ה', "_____," or _____, which means
to remove his shoes. (3:5)

ת _____ refers to the counted number of bricks. (5:18)

Answers

א, ב. אצטגניניו, בן

astrologers, son

ג. גבור בשליחותי

strong to fulfill My [Hashem's] mission

ד. דרך צרעת להיות לבנה

Tzaraas is normally white

ה. ההר הזה

This mountain

ו. וירא בסבלתם

[he] saw their suffering

ז. זקני ישראל, זקנים סתם, זקנים מיוחדים לישיבה

Elders of Yisrael, regular elderly people, Elders designated for counsel

ח. חמור מיוחד, חמור, חבש

special donkey, donkey, saddled

ט. טיט

י, כ. כולם, יראו ללכת

All of them, They were afraid to go forward

ל. להודיע חיבתם שנמשלו לכוכבים

So we know how much the Jewish people are beloved by Him because they are compared to the stars.

מ. מי אנכי, מה אני חשוב לדבר עם המלכים

Who am I, How am I important enough to speak with kings

נ. נולד, נתמלא הבית כולו אורה

born, The house was filled with light

ס. סוף

swampland

ע. עשה עצמו כאילו לא ידעו

He pretended as if he did not know who he was

פ, צ. פועה, צעקה

Puah, scream

ק. קולו כנער

His voice was like that of a child

ר. ריח רע

bad smell

ש. של נעליך, שלוף

Remove your shoes, slip off

ת. תכן לבנים

counted bricks

Questions

א   What does ערל שפתים mean? (6:12)

ב   The תורה says that there would be blood in all the land of מצרים which means, _____ and _____. (7:19)

ג, ד   How were the frogs placed after they died when the plague was over? (8:10)

ה   What is one piece of advice our Rabbis give to men prior to their getting married in order to choose the right mate? (6:23)

ו   By the plague of ערב, Hashem said, "_____," which means, "_____." (8:18)

ז   What was it that משה said that the מצרים hate about what בני ישראל do regarding their beliefs? (8:22)

ח   Where does the word שחין come from and what type of reaction does it cause? (9:9)

ט   The expression _____ means you are not yet fearful. (9:30)

י   ה׳ said He would stretch out His _____ on מצרים, which means _____, in order to strike them. (7:5)

כ   Why does ה׳ punish the sinful nations? (7:3)

ל   Why was משה excluded from actualizing מכת דם? (7:19)

ל, מ   Why did _____ insist that he would not pray to ה׳ until he would leave _____? (9:29)

נ   The שחין had fire inside of it which was a _____. (9:24)

ס   Which words refer to טורח משא מצרים – the burdens of מצרים? (6:6)

ע, פ, צ   It was because משה described himself as an _____ that ה׳ took אהרן as משה's _____ and that _____. (6:13)

ק   As long as even one of the שבטים were _____, there was no slavery. (6:16)

ר Hashem said that during the מכת דם, the מצריים will grow weary asking for a _____ for the water in order to have water that is _____. (7:17)

ש ה׳ referred to the מכת בכורות as "כל מגפותי" – all of My plagues. From this usage we learn _____. (9:14)

ת What is another word for snake? (7:9)

Answers

א. אטום שפתיים

sealed lips

ב. במרחצאות, באמבטאות שבבתים

bathhouses, baths in the homes

ג, ד. דגורין גלין

[They were] piled up like mounds

ה. הנושא אשה צריך לבדוק באחיה

One who gets married must research [the girl's] brother

ו. והפליתי, והפרשתי

I shall distinguish, I shall set apart

ז. זביחה שאנו זבחים

[The] sacrifice that we offer to sacrifice

ח. חמימות

heat

ט. טרם תיראון

not yet fearful

י. יד, יד ממש

hand, literally [His] hand

כ. כדי שישמעו ישראל וייראו

So that [Bnei Yisrael] will hear about the events and be fearful

ל. לפי שהגן היאור על משה כשנשלך לתוכו

Since the river protected Moshe when he was cast into it

ל, מ. משה, מן העיר, לפי שהיתה מלאה גלולים

Moshe, from the city, For it [the city] was filled with idolatry.

נ. נס בתוך נס

miracle within a miracle

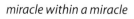

ס. סבלת מצרים

The burdens of Mitzrayim

ע, פ, צ. ערל שפתיים, פה, צרף לו הקדוש ברוך הוא את אהרן להיות לו לפה ולמליץ

blocked lips, mouth, Hashem joined Aharon together with him to help serve as his mouth and adviser

ק. קיים

surviving

ר. רפואה, ראויין לשתות

remedy, suitable for drinking

ש. שמכת בכורות שקולה כנגד כל המכות

that the slaying of the first born was equivalent (in hardship) to all of the plagues.

ת. תנין

snake

Questions

א, ב כל בכור בארץ The תורה says with regards to מכת בכורות that מצרים – every first born in the land of Egypt – would perish, including _____ and _____, as it says in Tehillim, למכה מצרים _____. (12:12)

ג The Aramaic word for כלה – completely. (11:1)

ד What is the way that a person is supposed to perform preparing the קרבן פסח? (12:11)

ה Who are the עם אשר ברגליך? (11:8)

ו The words את הבשר emphasize that בני ישראל were instructed to eat only the בשר of the sacrifice, _____. (12:8)

ז From these words, we learn that you should mention יציאת מצרים every day. (13:3)

ז, ח ארץ כנען is described as a land which is _____, flowing with milk and honey, as the _____, and similarly, the honey _____. (13:5)

ט תפילין are called _____ from the word _____, which means "two." (13:16)

י, כ When פרעה told משה that he did not want to see him anymore, משה responded, _____, which means_____. (10:29)

ל What do we learn from the words זכור את היום הזה אשר יצאתם ממצרים מבית עבדים? (13:3)

מ From what age is one considered a גבר? (12:37)

נ When one redeems a donkey for a lamb after entering ארץ כנען, _____. (13:13)

ס When is כחצות הלילה? (11:4)

ע משה told פרעה that he would leave מצרים _____.(11:8)

פ _____ was offered on the tenth of the month but not
_____. (12:3)

צ The קרבן פסח is supposed to be roasted ראשו על כרעיו, which means
_____. (12:9)

ק What was one of the wonders that ה׳ said He would increase to
impress פרעה and מצרים. (11:9)

ר הקדים refers to מזרחית and the _____ refers to _____.
(10:13,19)

ש Why was the night of יציאת מצרים referred to as ליל שמרים? (12:42)

ת This word means בלי מום – without blemish. (12:5)

Answers

א, ב. אף בכורות אחרים, אף בכורי מצרים שבמקומות אחרים, בבכוריהם
Even the firstborn of others [in Egypt], even firstborn of Egyptians who were not in Egypt [during the time of the plague], their firstborn

ג. גמירא
completely

ד. דרך דילוג וקפיצה
By way of skipping and jumping

ה. ההולכים אחר עצתך והלוכך
Those who follow your [Moshe's] advice and ways

ו. ולא גידים ועצמות
and not veins or bones

ז. זכור את היום הזה
remember this [specific] day

ז, ח. זבת חלב ודבש, חלב זב מן העזים, זב מן התמרים ומן התאנים
[that] flows with milk and honey, milk flows from the goats, flows from its dates and from its figs

ט. טוטפת, טט
totafot, "tat" [two]

י, כ. כן דברת, יפה דברת
yes you spoke, you spoke well

ל. למד שמזכירין יציאת מצרים בכל יום
We learn that you have to mention the exodus from Egypt every day.

מ. מבן עשרים שנה ומעלה
From twenty years of age and up

נ. נותן שה לכהן ופטר חמור מותר בהנאה

he gives a lamb to the Kohen and one can enjoy that which emerges first from the donkey

ס. סמוך לו

Close to it

ע. עם כל העם מארצך

with the entire nation from your land

פ. פסח מצרים, פסח דורות

Pessach [in] Egypt, Pessach [of future] generations

צ. צולהו כלו כאחד עם ראשו ועם כרעיו ועם קרבו

roast it all [all of its parts] as one unit together with its head, legs, and insides

ק. קריעת ים סוף

Splitting of the Reed Sea

ר. רוח ים, רוח מערבית

direction of the sea, in the direction of the west

ש. שהיה הקדוש ברוך הוא שומר ומצפה לו לקים הבטחתו להוציאם מארץ מצרים

Hakadosh Baruch Hu would watch and anticipate an opportunity to fulfill His promise to take [Bnei Yisrael] out from the land of Mitzrayim.

ת. תמים

wholesome [unblemished]

בשלח

Questions

א How far outside the תחום שבת is one allowed to stand? (16:29)

ב, ג _____ left מצרים _____, which means _____. (14:8)

ד The layer of טל that covered the מן was _____, which is a thin cover. (16:14)

ה The תורה says _____, which means that יוסף not only made his children swear to remove his bones from מצרים but also _____. (13:19)

ה, ו _____ means that אלוהים _____ . (13:18)

ז Which words demonstrate that ה' revealed Himself to בני ישראל and that they were able to point to Him with their finger? (15:2)

ח What did יהושע do to the strong men of עמלק? (17:13)

ט The מצריים _____, which became thick like _____. (15:4)

י What do we learn from the fact that משה told יהושע, his student, "choose men for *us*"? Explain. (17:9)

כ Which waters split during the קריעת ים סוף? (14:21)

ל, מ The color of the _____ was _____. (16:31)

נ What did ה' declare with regards to the nation of עמלק? (17:16)

ס This word means a marsh in which reeds grow. (13:18)

ע A type of measurement. (16:16)

פ בני ישראל camped in _____, whose name was changed to _____ because it was here that they became free men. The place was marked by two tall upright rocks and the valley in between was called _____. (14:2)

צ Dough which is fried with honey. (16:31)

ק עם ישראל demonstrated _____ when they complained about having no water. (15:25)

ר The _____ is the strongest of the _____ and it is the _____ used to exact punishment from _____. (14:21)

ש A type of bird which is very fat. (16:13)

ת ה׳ promised בני ישראל _____. (17:8)

בשלח

Answers

א. ארבע אמות

Four amot

ב, ג. בני ישראל, ביד רמה, בגבורה גבוהה ומפרסמת

Bnei Yisrael, with a raised hand, with great, renowned strength

ד. דבר דק

something thin

ה. השבע השביע, השביעם שישביעו לבניהם

he made [his children] swear, he made them swear that they, in turn, would have their children swear

ה, ו. ויסב, הסיבם מן הדרך הפשוטה לדרך העקומה

[He] took around, [He] took them around from the easier route to the winding route

ז. זה אלי

This is my God

ח. חתך ראשי גבוריו

He cut off the heads of their strong warriors

ט. טבעו בים, טיט

sank in the sea, cement

י. יהי כבוד תלמידך חביב עליך כשלך

The honor for one's student should be as dear to one as one's own.

By using the word "us," Moshe included Yehoshua, his student, in the same phrase and context as a leader of the Jewish people like himself.

כ. כל המים שבעולם

All the waters of the world

ל, מ. מן, לבן

Man, white

נ. נשבע הקדוש ברוך הוא שאין שמו שלם ואין כסאו שלם עד שימחה שמו של עמלק כלו

Hakadosh Baruch Hu swore that His name would not be complete nor would His throne be complete until the entire name and nation of Amalek would be completely erased and destroyed.

ס. סוף

marsh

ע. עומר

[type of] measurement

פ. פיתום, פי החירות, פי הסלעים

Pitom, Pi Hahirot, mouth of the rocks

צ. צפיחת

dough fried with honey

ק. קשי ערפו

[the nation's] stiff neck [brazenness]

ר. רוח קדים, רוחות, רוח, רשעים

east wind, winds, wind, wicked

ש. שליו

slav [type of bird]

ת. תמיד אני ביניכם ומזמן לכל צרכיכם

I can always be found amongst you and I am always prepared to help with all your needs.

Questions

א What is מצרים described as? (18:10)

ב The תורה uses the words _____ as opposed to the words _____ because it is more specific and refers to the appropriate time, which is _____. (19:1)

ג A מזבח of stones cannot be built _____, which is an expression of _____ or cutting. (20:22)

ד Why was יתרו referred to as חתן משה? (18:17)

ה משה instructed בני ישראל _____, which is the end of three days, in other words, _____, because _____. (19:15)

ו Which words in the פרשה demonstrate that בני ישראל encamped as one man with one heart? (19:2)

ז _____ are two statements that were said by ה׳ simultaneously (בדבור אחד). (20:8)

ח יתרו was also called _____ because he was _____. (18:1)

ט יתרו was happy about all the _____ that ה׳ did for בני ישראל, which refers to the _____. (18:9)

י How is one supposed to see things once שבת arrives? (20:9)

כ ה׳ told בני ישראל that they would be carried on _____, which means _____. (19:4)

ל _____ refers to kidnapping and _____ refers to stealing money. (20:13)

מ What do we learn from the words, את כל הדברים האלה? (20:1)

מ, נ Whenever the תורה uses the word _____, it refers to the _____ direction. (19:2)

ס At מעמד הר סיני, everyone was healed and even a _____ was able to see. (19:11)

ע The thickness of the clouds is referred to as the _____. (19:9)

פ How does the תורה refer to something which is sculpted? (20:4)

צ What turned hard as a pillar of marble? (18:4)

ק If ה׳, Who does not need rest, proclaimed that He rested on שבת, then
_____. (20:11)

ר The תורה says that בני ישראל at Har Sinai _____, which means
they miraculously were able to _____. (20:15)

ש What do we learn from the fact that the תורה says that יתרו returned
למשה ולישראל? (18:1)

ת ה׳ told בני ישראל with regard to the מזבח אדמה, _____, which
means that _____. (20:21)

יתרו

Answers

א. אומה קשה

A tough nation

ב. ביום הזה, ביום ההוא, בראש חודש

this day, on that day, first [day] of the month on

ג. גזית, גזיזה

gazit, cutting

ד. דרך כבוד קוראו הכתוב חותנו של מלך

The verse demonstrates respect [to Yitro] by referring to him as the father-in-law of the king [Moshe].

ה. היו נכונים לשלשת ימים, הוא יום רביעי, הוסיף משה יום אחד מדעתו

Prepare yourselves for three days, this was the fourth day, Moshe added one extra day based on his own calculation

ו. ויחן שם ישראל כנגד ההר

Bnei Yisrael encamped there next to the mountain.

ז. זכור ושמור

zachor veshamor (remember and adhere to)

ח. חובב, חבב את התורה

chovav, he loved the Torah

ט. טובה, טובת המן והבאר והתורה

kindness, the kindness [Hashem provided] by the Man, the water well, and the Torah

י. יהא בעיניך כאילו כל מלאכתך עשויה

It should appear to you as if all of your work is completed and done.

כ. כנפי נשרים, כנשר הנושא גוזליו על כנפיו

wings of an eagle, like an eagle who carries its offspring on its wings

ל. לא תגנב, לא תגנבו

you shall not steal, you [plural] shall not steal

מ. מלמד שאמר הקדוש ברוך הוא עשרת הדברות בדבור אחד

This teaches that Hakadosh Baruch Hu said all of the Ten Commandments in one statement.

מ, נ. נגד, מזרח

opposite, east

ס. סומא

blind person

ע. ערפל

fog

פ. פסל

sculpted idol

צ. צווארו של משה

Moshe's neck

ק. קל וחומר לאדם שמלאכתו בעמל ויגיעה שיהיה נח בשבת

how much more so does a person who toils and exerts effort in his work have to rest on Shabbat.

ר. רואין את הקולות, רואין את הנשמע

saw the voices, saw what can [normally only] be heard

ש. שקול משה כנגד כל ישראל

Moshe was equal to all of Yisrael

ת. תעשה לי, תהא תחלת עשיתו לשמי

make it for Me, the initial actions should already be in My name

Questions

א, ב   The words _____ demonstrate that people are punished if they hit their father or mother _____ and the punishment is death _____. Those who curse their father or mother are put to death _____. (21:15, 17)

ג   Someone who is born in a foreign country. (22:20)

ד   The תורה says _____, which means that one should not say, _____. (23:3)

ה   Which ear of the עבד עברי gets pierced should he choose to stay with his owner forever? (21:6)

ו   The word _____ means that משה sprinkled the blood. (24:8)

ז   What do the words שבעת ימים יהיה עם אמו serve as? (22:29)

ח, ט, י The expression _____ means that an animal was attacked and killed by a _____. In such a case, if _____, then he is exempt from paying the owner for the animal he was watching over. (22:12)

כ   In what way were the משפטים presented and organized in front of בני ישראל? (21:1)

ל   What is one of the first questions asked on the beginning of the פרשה? What is the answer given to this question? (21:1)

מ   Which important principal do we learn from the words כי גרים הייתם בארץ מצרים? (22:20)

נ   If it was _____ that a particular ox was _____ three times, and this ox kills another ox, the owner of such an ox has to pay _____. (21:36)

ס, ע   Someone who _____ has to give the חבר the value of his _____. (21:24)

ע From the word _____, we learn that if one has to choose between lending money to _____, then _____ is first. If one has to choose between lending money to an _____ or an _____, then the _____ is first; and if one has to choose between lending money to _____ and _____, then the _____ are first. (22:24)

פ Which two מצות does כל דברי ה' refer to? (24:3)

צ A type of שרץ. (23:28)

ק Someone who hits a _____ and kills him, is put to death, however a _____ who hits someone and kills them, is not put to death. (21:12)

ר The תורה instructs a judge, "אחרי _____" – this means that if _____ perverting justice, you should not decide to follow them simply because they are _____. (23:2)

ש ביכורים are taken from the _____ and even fruits grown during _____ must be offered for ביכורים. (23:19)

ת What happens to someone who takes a שוחד? (23:8)

Answers

א, ב. אביו ואמו, או זה או זה, בחנק, בסקילה

his father and mother, either this or that, through strangulation, through stoning

ג. גר

foreigner

ד. דל לא תהדר, דל הוא אזכנו ואכבדנו

do not glorify a destitute person, [do not say,] "He is destitute so I will find merit in his actions and I will honor him"

ה. הימנית

the right [ear]

ו. ויזרק

he threw [sprinkled]

ז. זו אזהרה לכהן שאם בא למהר את קרבנו לא ימהר קודם שמנה לפי שהוא מחסר זמן

This serves as a warning to the Kohen that in case he decides to speed up the sacrifice, he should not do so before [the animal's] eighth day because that would be lacking the minimal time.

ח, ט, י. טרף יטרף, חיה רעה, יביא עדים שנטרפה באונס

torn and mutilated, wild animal, [he] brings witnesses that it was mutilated by accident

כ. כשלחן הערוך ומוכן לאכול לפני האדם

Like a table which is set and prepared for the people in front of it to eat from.

ל. למה נסמכה פרשת דינין לפרשת מזבח, לומר לך שתשים סנהדרין אצל המקדש

Why is the section dealing with judicial cases adjacent to the section dealing with the Altar? To teach us that one is required to have a high court sit next to the Mikdash.

מ. מום שבך אל תאמר לחברך

Do not mention a flaw to a friend if you yourself have that flaw as well.

נ. נודע, נגח, נזק שלם

known, gored, full damages

ס, ע. סימא עין חבירו, עין

blinded his friend's eye, eye

ע. עמי, עמי ונכרי, עמי, עני, עשיר, עני, עניי עירך, עניי עיר אחרת, עניי עירך

My nation, "My" nation or[a] foreign nation, "My" nation, poor person, rich person, poor person, poor people from your city, poor people from a different city, poor people from your city

פ. פרישה והגבלה

Separating and Drawing boundaries

צ. צרעה

a type of insect

ק. קטן, קטן

minor, minor

ר. רבים להטות, ראית רשעים, רבים

lean according to the majority, [if] you see wicked people, majority

ש. שבעת המינים, שביעית

seven species, seventh year

ת. תטרף דעתו עליו וישתכח תלמודו ויכהה מאור עיניו

His mind will become confused and he will forget his learning and his eyes will be dimmed.

Questions

א _____ were placed on the _____ and the _____ were filling stones placed on the חושן. (25:7)

ב The lamps of the מנורה were like _____, and the oil and the wicks were placed _____. (25:37)

ג What was the height of both the interior מזבח and the outer מזבח, as compared to the length? (27:1)

ד The סירת were used to remove the _____ and the מזרקת were used to accept the _____. (27:3)

ה Another word for תרומה. (25:2)

ו The מסך in the משכן was a _____. (26:36)

ז Where are the loops on the panels of the משכן supposed to be positioned? (26:5)

ח What was the distance from pillar to pillar in the משכן? (27:14)

ט Which Babylonian poem states that the beams of the משכן were ready to be built? (26:15)

י The _____ served as a roof and an outside cover for the beams of the משכן. (26:1)

כ Which utensil in the משכן was made with the faces of creatures? (26:31)

ל Which words demonstrate that the תרומה should be given for ה's name? (25:2)

מ The יעות were _____, which were like covers of pots made out of _____. (27:3)

נ What were the pegs of the משכן shaped like? (27:19)

ס קרוב המזבח means _____. (27:5)

ע From the words _____, we learn that the משכן was _____ high. (26:16)

פ, צ The _____ on the מנורה refer to _____. (25:31)

צ What is תכלת and which color is it? (25:4)

ק A _____ of five panels is _____. The loops were made on the panel that was _____, which means _____ or outermost. (26:4)

ר What do the portions offered by בני ישראל for the משכן demonstrate? (25:2)

ש בצלאל made _____ and _____ were made from gold. (25:11)

ת The three types of _____ referred to at the beginning of the פרשה are _____, _____, and _____. (25:2)

Answers

א. אבני השהם, אפוד, אבני המלאים

the shoham stones, Eiphod, the filling stones

ב. בזיכין, בתוכן

bowls, inside of them

ג. גבהו פי שנים כארכו

Its height was twice its length

ד. דשן, דם

ashes, blood

ה. הפרשה

Something separated aside

ו. וילון

curtain

ז. זו כנגד זו

One corresponding to the next

ח. חמש אמות

Five amot (unit of measurement)

ט. טס מטע מזרזיים קורות בתינו ארזים

The planting of the roused [Israel] flew [from Egypt] to become the cedar beams of [our] Temple.

י. יריעות

curtains

כ. כרובים

Cherubs

ל. לי לשמי

For Me in My name

מ. מגרפות שנוטלים בהם את הדשן, מתכת דק

shovels which remove the ashes, [a] thin metal

נ. נגרי נחשת

Copper door bolts

ס. סביב

around

ע. עשר אמות אורך הקרש, עשר אמות

ten amot [breadths] was the height of the pole, ten amot [breadths]

פ, צ. פרחיה, ציורין עשוין בה

flowers, pictures made inside of them

צ. צמר צבוע בדם חלזון, צבעו ירוק

A wool that was colored with the blood of the chilazon, Its color was green

ק. קבוצה, קרויה חוברת, קיצונה, קצה

group, called a grouping, outer extreme, end

ר. רצון טוב

Good will

ש. שלושה ארונות, שנים מהם

three Arks, two of them

ת. תרומות, תרומת בקע לגלגלת, תרומת המזבח, תרומת המשכן

portions, a portion [of a certain amount] per head, portion toward the Mizbeach, portion toward the Mishkan

תצוה

Questions

א The _____ on the איפוד were set according to _____ and the order of the _____ were according to the order in which the שבטים were born, for example, the first stone was _____, the stone of ראובן. (28:21)

ב One of the requirements of the שמן זית used in the משכן was that it must be _____. (27:20)

ג What did the מזבח הקטורת have that the מזבח העולה did not? (30:3)

ד The מנורה had to have enough oil in it to ensure that it would remain _____. (27:21)

ה What is the חטאת הכפרים? (30:10)

ו The subject of the words _____ refers to אהרן and his sons. (29:33)

ז What kind of bells were on the מעיל of the כהן גדול? (28:33)

ח The _____ was a תבשיט כנגד הלב and the מעיל was a type of _____. (28:4)

ט The ציץ was like a _____, which was two finger-breadths wide. (28:36)

י What were figuratively filled for the inauguration and appointment to the כהונה? (29:9)

כ The stones on the אפד, which represented the שבטים, were arranged _____, which means _____. (28:11)

ל, מ, נ The words _____ mean that the _____ would _____. (27:20)

מ The stones that filled the חשן were called _____ because they were _____ the spaces and settings carved around them. (28:17)

נ What is another name for the ציץ? (29:6)

ס, ע   The קטורת consisted of _____, which caused _____. (30:1)

פ   What was the whole courtyard of the משכן referred to as? (29:32)

צ   _____ means _____ of its sides. (30:4)

ק   What did the כהן arrange around the אפוד? (29:5)

ר   The bells on the כהן's coat were called _____ because they were round and hollow like _____. (28:3)

ש   The _____ were _____, which are gold chains. (28:14)

ת   What is the חשן? (28:4)

Answers

א. אבנים, איש על שמו, אבנים, אודם

stones, each man according to his name, stones, Odem

ב. בלי שמרים

without sediment

ג. גג

roof

ד. דולקת מערב ועד בקר

[remain] lit from the evening through until the morning

ה. הם פר ושעיר של יום הכפורים המכפרים על טמאת מקדש וקדשיו

These are the bull and the goat of Yom Hakippurim, which atone for impurity of the Mikdash and its sacred utensils.

ו. ואכלו אותם

they ate them

ז. זגין עם ענבלין שבתוכם

Bells with clappers inside of them

ח. חושן, חלוק

breastplate, cloak

ט. טס של זהב

golden plate

י. יד אהרן, יד בניו

Aharon's hand, [Aharon's] children's hands

כ. כתולדתם, כסדר שנולדו

according to their births, according to the order in which they were born

ל, מ, נ. להעלת נר תמיד, נרות, מדליק עד שתהא שלהבת עולה מאליה

to light a constant candle light, candles, [it would] be lit until the flame of the candle would stand on its own

מ. מלואים, ממלאות

filler, filling in

נ. נזר הקודש

crown of sanctity

ס, ע. סמים, עשן

spices, smoke

פ. פתח אוהל מועד

The opening of the Ohel Moed

צ. צלעתיו, צדיו

[its] corners, [its] sides

ק. קשט ותקן החגורה והסנר סביבותיו

He decorated and fixed the belt and apron around it.

ר. רימונים, רימונים

pomegranates, pomegranates

ש. שרשרת זהב, שלשלאות

chains of gold, chains

ת. תכשיט כנגד הלב

An ornament next to [his] heart

Questions

א שבת is an _____ and so the תורה warns _____, which is a warning that _____. (31:13)

ב How did the כהנים wash their hands and feet? (30:19)

א, ב A person who is מחלל שבת is put to death _____; however, _____, a מחלל שבת receives כרת. (31:14)

ג, ד A description of the כיור. (30:18)

ה What did 'ה do for משה to demonstrate to him what the מחצית השקל was? (30:13)

ו What are two ways of saying "and He rested"? (31:17)

ז If בני ישראל rebel against 'ה, then 'ה will show _____ toward them. (33:3)

ח, ט _____ is the amount of money that has to be given for פדיון הבכור and the _____ is the only בהמה _____ that requires to be redeemed. (34:20)

י _____ is spelled with two _____ to emphasize the prohibition against the act of using oils which belong to הקדש. (30:32)

כ The word _____ is written _____ in the תורה to demonstrate that 'ה gave the תורה to משה as a gift much like a חתן would give a special gift to his _____. (31:18)

ל What does 'ה promise to those who subscribe to אמת? (34:6)

מ One who is _____ is like someone who is _____. (33:7)

נ, ס משה made בני ישראל drink following the חטא העגל because _____ just like _____. (32:20)

ע Which word teaches us that ארץ ישראל is the highest of all lands? (33:1)

פ, צ   אהרן told בני ישראל, "_____," which was a _____. (32:2)

ק   What did ה׳ show משה from behind? (33:23)

ר   ה׳ said that He filled בצלאל with _____. This includes knowledge that refers to _____. (31:3)

ש   What did ה׳ warn regarding the production of the קטרת? (30:37)

ת   ה׳ instructed משה to write down these words (exclusively). From here we learn that one should not write down _____. (34:27)

Answers

א. אות גדולה, אך את שבתתי תשמרו, אף על פי שתהיו רדופין וזריזין בזריזות המלאכה שבת אל תדחה מפניה

great sign, just observe My Shabbats, even though you will be pursuing your livelihood earnestly and you are immersed in your work do not push off the Shabbat because of the work you have

ב. בבת אחת היה מקדש ידיו ורגליו

They washed their hands and legs simultaneously.

א, ב. אם יש עדים והתראה, בלא התראה

If there are [both]witnesses and warning, without warning

ג, ד. דוד גדולה

A large kettle

ה. הראה לו כמין מטבע של אש ומשקלה מחצית השקל ואמר לו כזה יתנו

[Hashem] showed [Moshe] like a coin of fire whose weight was [like that of] half a shekel, and He said, "This is what they shall give".

ו. וינפש, ונח

rested, and rested

ז. זעם

anger

ח, ט. חמישה סלעים מכל מין ומין, חמור, טמאה

[the value of] five selaim from every type, donkey, impure

י. ייסך, יודין

smear, two letter yuds

כ. ככלותו, ככלתו, כלה

upon completion, like his bride, bride

ל. לשלם שכר טוב לעושי רצונו

reward those who fulfill His will

מ. מבקש פני זקן, מקבל פני השכינה

one who seeks out the presence of an elderly person, accepts the Divine presence [of Hashem]

נ, ס. נתכון לבודקן, סוטות

[he] intended to check them, sotot [women accused of an adulterous relationship]

ע. עלה

come up

פ, צ. פרקו נזמי זהב, ציווי

remove your gold jewelry, command

ק. קשר של תפילין

The knot of [His] Tefillin

ר. רוח אלהים, רוח הקדש

Godly spirit, Divine inspiration

ש. שלא תעשנה אלא לשמי

[that] it should only be made for My name

ת. תורה שבעל פה

the oral law

Questions

ד, ג, ב, א _____, who was from _____, one of the lowest שבטים, was granted the same status as _____, who was from לוי, one of the _____, with regard to working on the משכן. (35:34)

ה What did משה present to בני ישראל before he explained the work involved in the משכן? (35:2)

ו What happened on the day after יום הכפורים? (35:1)

ז, ח The _____ was a round piece of jewelry made of _____, which was worn on the _____. (35:22)

ח What were the מיתרים and what were they used for in the משכן? (35:18)

ט What did the women do that involved the fleece from on the back of the goats? (35:26)

י What does the word משכן refer to? (35:11)

כ The _____ was a _____ and ornament, which was donated by the women for the אהל מועד. (35:22)

ל What were the בגדי השרד used for? (35:19)

מ Two utensils used to service the מנורה. (35:14)

נ Since the _____ were lazy, _____, and their title name was written "_____," without a י. (35:27)

ס The word מסך is related to the word _____, referring to the פרוכת used as a partition. (35:12)

ע Why are those who give portions of money for the משכן referred to as a נדיב לב? (35:5)

פ The _____ was a _____, which was used to protect the משכן. (35:12)

צ   What did the women establish by using mirrors in מצרים? (38:8)

ק   The מסך שער החצר had the same measurements as the _____. (38:18)

ר   The נבוב לחת were made of עצי שיטים that spread out toward every _____. (38:7)

ש   What did the כיור and כנו encourage? (38:8)

ת   The לחם הפנים had surfaces and stood vertically like a _____. (35:13)

ויקהל

Answers

א, ב, ג, ד. אהליאב, דן, בצלאל, גדולי השבטים
Ahaliav, [the tribe of] Dan, Betzalel, greatest of the tribes

ה. הקדים להם אזהרת שבת
He first introduced to them the prohibition against working on Shabbat.

ו. ויקהל משה את כל עדת בני ישראל
Moshe assembled the entire congregation of Bnei Yisrael.

ז, ח. חח, זהב, זרוע
chach, gold, forearm

ח. חבלים לקשור
ropes used for tying

ט. טוו את העיזים
Spun [the fleece from] the goats.

י. יריעות התחתונות הנראות בתוכו
The lower panels, which were visible from within the Mishkan

כ. כומז, כלי זהב
kumaz, gold piece

ל. לכסות הארון והשלחן והמנורה והמזבחות בשעת סילוק מסעות
To cover the Aron, Table, Menorah, and Altars during the time of departures for journeying

מ. מלקחים, מחתות
Tongs, Scoops

נ. נשיאים, נחסרה אות משמם, נשאים
princes, a letter is missing from their title, princes [without the letter yud]

ס. סכך
cover

ע. על שם שלבו נודבו

Due to the fact that it was their hearts that contributed.

פ. פרוכת המסך, פרוכת המחיצה

parochet screen, parochet partition wall

צ. צבאות רבות

Many legions

ק. קלעי החצר

curtains of the courtyard

ר. רוח

direction

ש. שלום בין איש לאישתו

Peace between husband and wife

ת. תיבה פרוצה

open box

Questions

א   How did משה offer a bracha to בני ישראל? (39:43)

ב   What is the weight of a half shekel? (38:26)

ג   What are the edges of the חשן called? (39:15)

ד   The normal _____ was with _____, as was done with the חשן and the אפד. (39:31)

ה   What happened in each place that בני ישראל journeyed to? (40:38)

ו   One of the ברכות that משה offered to בני ישראל was, "_____." (39:43)

ז   One of the materials used for the משכן that are counted in the פרשה is _____. (38:21)

ח   What were used to fasten the ציץ onto the מצנפת? (39:31)

ט   How was the gold of the אפד flattened out? (39:3)

י   What does the אהל which was spread out over the משכן refer to? (40:19)

כ   No one managed to build the משכן because of _____. (39:33)

ל, מ   There were two _____ of the _____. (40:4)

נ   When _____, משה would _____ with ה'. (40:35)

ס   A word which refers to protection. (40:3)

ע   The משכן העדות was _____ that ה' forgave them _____. (38:21)

פ   A screen used to protect the ארון. (40:3)

צ   The word ירך is translated as _____, which means side (40:22)

ק   The _____ was offered both שחרית and ערבית. (40:27)

ש, ר   The word משכן appears _____ in the opening פסוק of the פרשה as a _____. (38:21)

ת   The hats made for the כהנים are described as the _____. (39:28)

Answers

א. אמר להם יהי רצון שתשרה שכינה במעשה ידיכם

He said to them, "May it be the will [of Hashem] that His presence should rest upon the work of your hands".

ב. בקע

Beka

ג. גבלת

gevulot

ד. דרך קשירה, ד' חוטין

the normal manner of tying, four strings

ה. היה הענן שוכן במקום אשר יחנו שם

The cloud would reside any place where they camped.

ו. ויהי נעם אדני אלהינו עלינו

the pleasantness of Hashem our God should rest upon us

ז. זהב

gold

ח. חוטי תכלת

Blue strings

ט. טסין היו מרדדין מן הזהב

They would beat plates from the gold.

י. יריעות העיזים

Panels of goats' skins

כ. כובד הקרשים

The heavy weight of the beams

ל, מ. מערכות, לחם הפנים

stacks, bread of surfaces

נ. נסתלק הענן, נכנס ומדבר

presence of the cloud lifted, [he would] enter and speak

ס. סכת

protected

ע. עדות לישראל, על מעשה העגל

testimony for Yisrael, regarding the [idolatrous] act of the golden calf

פ. פרוכת

screen

צ. צידה

side

ק. קטורת

incense

ר, ש. שני פעמים, רמז למקדש שנתמשכן בשני חורבנין על עונותיהן של ישראל

two times, alludes to the Mikdash, which became collateral through the destruction of both Temples because of the sins of Yisrael

ת. תפארת המגבעות

the splendid hats

וַיִּקְרָא

Vayikra

Questions

א Which word demonstrates that 'ה spoke specifically to משה and not to אהרן? (1:1)

ב The תורה says _____, which teaches us that one must offer _____ and not חיות for a קרבן. (1:2)

ג Which part of the animal is the עורף? (5:8)

ד What is the sweetness of a fruit called? (2:11)

ה Which portion of money does בראשו refer to? (5:24)

ו A language which demonstrates affection and is used by the מלאכי השרת. (1:1)

ז, ח When performing _____ for a _____, the כהן uses his finger, as opposed to all other sacrifices, when he is _____ with a utensil. (4:8)

ח These words demonstrate that one has to offer a sacrifice with proper intentions. (4:24)

ט When the תורה refers to _____, it is referring to _____. (5:3)

י A process done to all of the מנחות. (2:6)

כ The כהן sprinkled the blood toward the פרוכת, which was _____. (4:6)

ל The word גרש is a _____. (2:14)

מ, נ What are two types of animals which are forbidden to be offered as קרבנות? (1:2)

נ The first type of קרבנות listed in the פרשה are _____. (1:2)

ס, ע The תורה says _____, which refers to the _____. (4:13)

ע, פ   If a כהן גדול does his _____ while wearing the clothing of a כהן הדיוט, then _____. (1:7)

צ   What does the כהן use in order to perform the process of מליקה? (1:15)

ק   Eastern direction. (1:16)

ר   The מנחה מרחשת is prepared in a deep pan and it seems _____ because it mixes with a lot of liquid, which causes it to appear as if it is _____. (2:7)

ש   What are the two explanations as to why one of the קרבנות is referred to as a שלמים? (3:1)

ת   Name two types of fruits that are offered for בכורים? (2:12)

Answers

א. אליו

to him

ב. בקר וצאן, בהמות

cattle and flocks, animals

ג. גובה הראש המשפע לצד הצואר

The top part of the head, which bends toward the neck.

ד. דבש

honey

ה. הוא הקרן ראש הממון

It is the principal or "head of money" that one must return after stealing or finding an item.

ו. ויקרא

He summoned

ז, ח. זריקת הדם, חטאת, זורק

sprinkling of blood, "Chatat" sacrifice, sprinkle

ח. חטאת הוא

it is a Chatat sacrifice

ט. טמאת אדם, טמאת מת

impurity of a man, impurity from a dead person

י. יציקה

pouring

כ. כנגד מקום קדשתה, כנגד בין הבדים

opposite the place of holiness, opposite the place between the poles [of the Aron]

ל. לשון שבירה וטחינה

language [that describes] breaking and grinding

מ, נ. מקצה, נעבד

an animal designated for idol worship, an animal used for idol worship

נ. נדבה

donated offerings

ס, ע. עדת ישראל, סנהדרין

assembly of Yisrael, Sanhedrin (high court of justice)

ע, פ. עבודה, עבודתו פסולה

service, [his] service is invalid

צ. צפרניו

his fingernail

ק. קדמה

east

ר. רך, רוחש ומנענע

soft, crawling and moving

ש. שמטילים שלום בעולם, שיש בהם שלום למזבח ולכהנים ולבעלים

they instill peace in the world, they bring peace to the mizbeach and to the Kohanim and to those who brought the sacrifice

ת. תאנים, תמרים

figs, dates

Questions

א Someone who eats פיגול, _____ in which it is acceptable to consume a sacrifice, is still considered a sinner. (7:18)

ב The כהנים are instructed to eat the מצות _____, which is _____. (6:9)

ג A word which refers to ה' is _____. (6:16)

ד The _____ of birds and animals is forbidden but _____ is permissible. (7:26)

ה Which function on the מזבח is כשר to execute all night? (6:2)

ו These words praise אהרן and his sons for doing exactly as they were instructed. (8:36)

ז, ח The word צו is a command for the sake of _____, which urges people on, particularly in מצות that cause _____. (6:2)

ט Someone who is _____ and eats a קרבן that is _____ does not receive כרת. (7:20)

י Which פסוק in תהילים demonstrates that one is obligated to give thanks to ה'? (7:12)

כ At what point is the כהן obligated to remove the dirt from the מזבח? (6:4)

ל, מ _____ wore a cloak that was _____ for the entire seven days of the inauguration. (8:28)

נ The continual fire that burned on the מזבח was used to light _____ and was referred to as the _____. (6:6)

ס A קרבן slaughtered with no intent is called שחיטת _____. (7:5)

ע Which קרבן was offered first every day? (6:5)

פ, צ _____ were set inside the _____. (8:9)

ק ה' instructed משה, "_____," which meant _____. (8:2)

ר משה anointed אהרן by pouring oil first on his _____ and then between _____. (8:12)

ש Why did the כהן remove his בגדי כהונה before he cleaned the מזבח? (6:4)

ת The words "_____" teach us that _____ and that all the קרבנות מנחה had to be mixed with oil and frankincense. (6:7)

Answers

א. אפילו בתוך הזמן

even within the time frame

ב. במקום קדוש, בחצר אהל מועד

in a holy place, in the courtyard of the Ohel Moed [Tent of Meeting]

ג. גבוה

high

ד. דם, דם דגים וחגבים

blood, fish blood and grasshopper's blood

ה. הקטר חלבים ואיברים

Burning of innards and body parts

ו. ויעש אהרן ובניו

Aharon and his sons did

ז, ח. זירוז, חסרון כיס

encouragement, financial loss

ט. טהור, טמא

pure, impure

י. יודו לה׳ חסדו ונפלאותיו לבני אדם

"Give thanks to Hashem for His kindness and for the wonders He provides for mankind".

כ. כשהוא הרבה ואין מקום למערכה

When the ashes have collected a lot and there is no room to place wood on the Mizbeach.

ל, מ. משה, לבן

Moshe, white

נ. נרות, נר תמיד

candles, continuous flame

ס. סתם

with no purpose

ע. עולת תמיד

The continual Olah offering

פ, צ. פתילי תכלת, ציץ

strands of blue, Tzitz

ק. קח את אהרן, קחנו בדברים ומשכהו

take Aharon, take him with words and persuade him

ר. ראש, ריסי עיניו

head, his eyelashes

ש. שלא ילכלך בהוצאת הדשן בגדים שהוא משמש בהן תמיד

In order that the clothing, which he regularly uses [in service], should not become soiled as he removes the ashes.

ת. תורת המנחה, תורה אחת לכולן

rules regarding the Mincha sacrifice, all the sacrifices shared the same guidelines

Questions

א _____, _____, and _____ were all instructed, "_____" their heads, which means _____. From here we learn that normally, an _____. (10:6)

ב What did אהרן say in order to bless בני ישראל? (9:22)

ג A snake is an example of an animal that walks on its _____. (11:42)

ד In which way is it אסור for a כהן to drink wine as he is entering and while he is serving in the אוהל מועד? (10:9)

ה Which category of water cannot become impure? (11:36)

ו The word _____ obligates us to sanctify ourselves in this world, and the words, "_____" teach us that ה' will sanctify us from the heavens for עולם הבא. (11:44)

ז Which מנחה did משה instruct אהרן and his sons to eat? (10:12)

ח There were only two קרבן _____ that were _____, which means their blood was sprinkled on the outer מזבח. (9:11)

ט Even if only the _____ of a non-kosher animal is mixed into a food and is evident, it is אסור to eat the mixture. (11:11)

י One of the blessings that משה and אהרן offered to בני ישראל during the שבעת ימי המלואים. (9:23)

כ, ל משה told אהרן to inform בני ישראל to take קרבנות, _____, which means that ה' intended _____. (9:4)

מ, נ The פסוק, "_____" demonstrates how fearful ה' is when He judges צדיקים because חזל change the word _____ to _____, which means, "God is feared from His sanctified ones – the צדיקים." (10:3)

ס What does a fish use to swim? (11:9)

ע אהרן would only enter the משכן to work _____. (9:1)

פ What was said specifically by ה׳ directly to אהרן (without mentioning משה)? (10:3)

צ One of the criteria for an animal to be kosher is that its entire hoof has to be split into two _____. (11:3)

ק What did אהרן receive for remaining silent after hearing about the death of his two sons? (10:3)

ר, ש The day that was _____ turned out to fall on _____. (9:1)

ת Name a non-kosher animal that is similar to a mouse and that flies at night. (11:18)

Answers

א. אהרן, אלעזר, איתמר, אל תפרעו, אל תגדלו שער, אבל אסור בתספורת

Aharon, Elazar, Itamar, do not leave your heads unkempt, do not grow your hair, one who is in mourning is not aloud to cut his hair

ב. ברכת כהנים

The priestly blessing

ג. גיחון

belly

ד. דרך שכרותו

in a drunken state

ה. המחברים לקרקע

That which is connected to the ground

ו. והתקדשתם, והייתם קדושים

sanctify yourselves, and you should be holy

ז. זו מנחת שמיני ומנחת נחשון

This is the meal offering of the eighth day and the meal offering of Nachshon.

ח. חטאת, חטאת חיצונה

sin offering, sin offering outside [its blood is sprinkled on the outer mizbeach.[

ט. טעם

taste

י. יהי רצון שתשרה שכינה במעשה ידיכם

May it be the will [of Hashem] that His divine presence should rest upon the work of your hands.

כ, ל. כי היום יהוה נראה אליכם, להשרות שכינתו במעשה ידיכם

for today Hashem will appear to you, [He] will rest His divine presence upon the work of your hands

שמיני

מ, נ. נורא אלהים ממקדשיך, ממקדשיך, ממקדשיך

God is feared from Your Sanctuary, from Your Sanctuary, from Your sanctified ones

ס. סנפיר

fins

ע. על פי הדבור

through the word [meaning the invitation] of Hashem

פ. פרשת שתויי יין

The directives regarding drinking wine

צ. צפרנין

nails

ק. קבל שכר על שתיקתו

He was rewarded for remaining silent.

ש, ר. שמיני למלואים, ראש חדש ניסן

eighth day of the inauguration, first of the month of Nissan

ת. תנשמת

tinshamet

Questions

א Once a woman has waited thirty-three days to become pure after giving birth, she remains pure _____. (12:4)

ב _____ is a type of affliction, which got its name from the word _____. (13:2)

ג How do we know that only a כהן can declare if a person is טמא from טהור or צרעת? (13:2)

ד, ה _____ is an expression referring to something _____, which makes the woman טמא. (12:2)

ו, ז The word _____ demonstrates that only one thing obstructs a woman who is טמא from eating קדשים; What is the special קרבן she has to offer? (12:7)

ח What does שחין cause to one's body? (13:18)

ט Before a garment is purified, it has to be washed, which refers to _____. (13:58)

י The final letter ה in the words, "_____" is pronounced because the תורה is emphasizing _____. (12:4)

כ Why does the פרשה of תזריע immediately follow the פרשה about kosher animals? (12:2)

כ, ל, מ The word _____ is written _____ that even if a woman gives birth to a _____, she is still טמא. (12:2)

נ, ס If the appearance of a _____ is not deeper than the skin, then the מצורע has to shave _____ and wait another seven days. (13:33)

ע What does the word תשב always mean? (12:4)

פ If the affliction _____ during the first week, then the מצורע is definitely טמא. (13:5)

ק, צ, פ   The garments of someone who has _____ are _____, which means they are _____. (13:45)

ר   What is צרבת שחין? (13:23)

ש   The מצורע has to grow a _____, which is the _____. (13:45)

ת   An example of something sacred that is forbidden for the woman who is impure to touch. (12:4)

Answers

א. אף על פי שרואה דם

even though she sees blood

ב. בהרת, בהיר

baheret, cloudy

ג. גזרת הכתוב היא שאין טמאת נגעים וטהרתן אלא על פי הכהן

It is a decree that declaring an affliction pure or impure can only be done by the word of the Kohen.

ד, ה. דוותה, הזב מגופה

infirmity, [something] which flows from her body

ו, ז. והקריבו, זה חטאת

and shall offer sacrifice, this is a sin offering

ח. חימום

heat

ט. טבילה

immersion

י. ימי טהרה, ימי טהר שלה

her days of purity, the days of her [specific] purity

כ. כשם שיצירתו של אדם אחר כל בהמה חיה ועוף במעשה בראשית כך תורתו נתפרשה אחר תורת בהמה חיה ועוף

Just like the creation of man was listed in Creation after the creation of the animals, beasts, and birds, so, too, the laws [regarding man] are listed after those regarding animals, beasts, and birds.

כ, ל, מ. כי, לרבות, מחוי

when, to include, liquefied

נ, ס. נתק, סביבות הנתק

netek, around the netek

ע. עכבה

staying

פ. פשה

spread[s]

פ, צ, ק. צרעת, פרמים, קרועים

tzaraat, torn, torn

ר. רשם שחנא, רשם החימום

mark of inflammation, mark inflamed from heat

ש. שפם, שיער שפתיים

mustache, hair growing over the lips

ת. תרומה

Trumah

Questions

א What does the תורה expect the כהן to rule about regarding the
מצורע? (14:57)

ב, ג The affliction of צרעת _____ because of _____. (14:4)

ד The כהן places spring water in the vessel before he slaughters the bird
for the purification of the מצורע in order that the _____ should
be recognizable. (14:5)

ה What kind of act does a זב have to do to pottery to make it impure?
(15:12)

ו, ז A _____ is different, _____, because _____,
_____. (15:25)

ח The כהן would venture _____ in order to check the status of the
מצורע. (14:3)

ח, ט The word _____ comes to exclude _____. (14:4)

י Name one of the ways a person rectifies his behavior from getting
צרעת. (14:4)

כ, ל When the תורה says that the כהן sprinkled the oil or blood
_____, it means that he did so _____. (14:16)

ל Why did ה' inform בני ישראל that He was going to afflict the houses
that they would posses from the כנענים with צרעת? (14:34)

מ, נ The _____ was placed in front of the gate
called _____ during his purification. (14:11)

ס At what point does the כהן come to check if afflictions have spread in
someone's house? (14:43)

ע Even someone who sits _____ of a נדה or _____ of a נדה,
is also required to immerse his clothing in the מקוה to purify them.
(15:23)

פ Another word for נזירה is _____, which means separated. (15:31)

צ, ק The מצורע is afflicted with צרעת because he spoke slander. Therefore he is required to offer _____ as part of his sacrifice because _____ constantly use their mouths and chirp with _____. (14:4)

ר How much water is in the utensil as the כהן slaughters one of the birds into it during the purification of the מצורע? (14:5)

ש How many days does the תורה mean when it refers to the ימים רבים that a woman's blood flows? (15:25)

ת Even a _____ cannot declare if there is an affliction on his house. Only the כהן can make that determination. (14:35)

Answers

א. איזה יום מטהרו ואיזה יום מטמאו

On which day he declares his purity and on which day he declares his impurity.

ב, ג. באין, גסות רוח

comes, haughtiness

ד. דם ציפור

blood of the bird

ה. היסיט

[He must] move it.

ו, ז. זבה, ולא כדת הנדה, זו טעונה ספירת שבעה נקיים וקרבן, והנדה אינה
טעונה ספירת שבעה נקיים

*zavah, not like [the laws] of a woman impure from menstruation, this one re-
quires counting seven clean days and offering a sacrifice but the woman impure
from menstruation does not require counting seven clean days*

ח. חוץ לשלשה מחנות

outside of three camps

ח, ט. חיות, טרפות

*live animals, tereifot [animals with physical defects which will inevitably result in
their death]*

י. ישפיל עצמו מגאותו

He [should] lower himself from his haughtiness.

כ, ל. לפני יהוה, כנגד בית קדשי הקדשים

in front of Hashem, opposite the place of the Holy of Holies

ל. לפי שהטמינו אמוריים מטמוניות של זהב בקירות בתיהם כל ארבעים שנה
שהיו ישראל במדבר ועל ידי הנגע נותץ הבית ומוצאן

*Because the Amorites hid treasures of gold in the walls of their houses during the
forty years that Bnei Yisrael were in the desert and the affliction of tzaraat would
break down the walls of the house and expose the treasure for Bnei Yisrael to find.*

מ, נ. מצורע, ניקנור

metzora, Nikanor

ס. סוף השבוע

week's end

ע. על משכב, על מושב

on the bed, on the seat

פ. פרישה

separated

צ, ק. צפורים, צפורים, צפצוף קול

birds, birds, chirping

ר. רביעית

Reviit (quarter)

ש. שלושה ימים

Three days

ת. תלמיד חכם

wise scholar

Questions

א When the תורה refers to the sacrifices of בני ישראל _____, it is referring to the sacrifices _____. (17:5)

ב Who is the תורה warning to safeguard בני ישראל from abominable practices? (18:30)

ב, ג The _____ of the word _____ is 410, alluding to the _____, which stood for 410 years. (16:3)

ד How was the קטורת that was offered on יום כיפור prepared? (16:12)

ה What kind of place was עזאזל? (16:8)

ו "_____" demonstrates that אהרן had one animal stand to his right and another animal stand to his left, _____. (16:8)

ז The תורה says, ומזרעך לא תתן להעביר למלך. What does the word "להעביר" (to pass) refer to? (18:21)

ח One of the places where it is prohibited to offer sacrifices. (17:3)

ט On יום כיפור the כהן is _____, which happens five times. (16:4)

י What did ה' instruct משה to warn אהרן about regarding coming to the קודש? (16:2)

כ, ל חקים are decrees from ה', _____ and _____. (18:4)

ל Why was the כהן גדול prohibited from entering the קודש on יום כיפור with gold garments? Explain. (16:4)

מ When אהרן brought his חטאת, what would he do to atone for himself and his household? (16:7)

נ Blood is the main source that allows the _____ to exist. (17:14)

ס, ע Someone who follows the מצות is promised a long life, which must refer to _____ because the result of _____ is _____. (18:5)

ע ארץ ישראל cannot tolerate _____. (18:28)

פ ה' said that He would direct "_____" toward anyone who consumes blood of an animal, which means "_____." (17:10)

צ עזאזל was a _____. (16:8)

ק Types of relationships that are prohibited from the תורה. (18:17)

ר One of the requirements for someone who eats a נבלה or טרפה. (17:16)

ש Why was אהרן warned about approaching the קדש immediately following his sons' demise? What would be the consequence should אהרן decide to approach the קדש at the wrong time? (16:1, 2)

ת The blood of an animal is offered as atonement on the מזבח because _____. (17:11)

Answers

א. אשר הם זבחים, אשר הם רגילים לזבח

that they slaughter, that they are accustomed to slaughter

ב. בית דין

Bet Din (court of justice)

ב, ג. גמטריא, בזאת, בית ראשון

numerical value, with this, First Temple

ד. דקה מן הדקה

Extra fine

ה. הוא הר עז וקשה

It is a very stiff and hard mountain.

ו. ונתן אהרן על שני השעירים גרלות, ונותן שתי ידיו בקלפי ונוטל גורל בימין וחברו בשמאל ונותן עליהם את שכתוב בו לשם הוא לשם ואת שכתוב בו לעזאזל משתלח לעזאזל

and Aharon will place the lots on the two goats, and he will place both his hands in the box and draw one lot in his right hand and the second lot in his left and he places the lots on the goats and on ,whichever one written, "to Hashem" is to Hashem and on whichever one written, "to Azazel" will go to Azazel.

ז. זו היא מסירתו לכומרים

This [refers to] transferring over to the priests

ח. חוץ לעזרה

Outside the Azara (hall of the Mikdash)

ט. טעון טבילה בכל חליפותיו

requires immersion [in the mikva] every time he changes his garments

י. יזהר שלא ירגיל לבא

He should be careful not to come regularly

כ, ל. כגון אכילת חזיר, לבישת שעטנז

such as eating pork, wearing shaatnes

ל. לפי שאין קטיגור נעשה סניגור

because a prosecutor does not become a defender

   The Kohen Gadol does not wear gold on Yom Kippur because when he is pleading for the defense of the Jewish people and asking for them to be forgiven for their sins, gold would remind Hashem of the Golden Calf, which is reason to prosecute Bnei Yisrael for having worshiped it.

מ. מתודה עליו עונותיו ועונות ביתו

[He] atoned for himself his sins and the sins of his household.

נ. נפש

body

ס, ע. עולם הבא, עולם הזה, סופו הוא מת

world to come, this world, in the end he dies

ע. עוברי עבירה

sinners

פ. פנאי, פונה אני מכל עסקי ועוסק בו

My attention, I will turn aside from all of My business and deal with him

צ. צוק גבוה

high cliff

ק. קרובות זו לזו

Relations close to one another

ר. רחיצת גופו

Washing his body

ש. שלא ימות כדרך שמתו בניו, שאם בא הוא מת

So that he should not die the same way his sons did, for if he comes he would die.

ת. תבוא נפש ותכפר על הנפש

the soul [of the animal] will come and atone for the soul [of the man]

Questions

א The מצוה of שבת is in the same פסוק as the obligation to fear the מקדש in order to teach us that _____. (19:30)

ב The תורה says to differentiate _____, which means that we are expected to differentiate _____ and also _____. (20:25)

ג The word הערה means _____ and all ערוה relates to _____ and improper exposure. (20:18)

ד Before בני ישראל would consider worshiping עבודה זרה, Hashem beseeched them, "_____." (19:31)

ה What does קדושים תיהיו mean? (19:1)

ו, ז Whatdoestheתורה'scommand,_____,teachandemphasize? (20:7)

ח What kind of death does the Torah refer to when the word מיתה is used without specification? (20:10)

ט If a person sees someone _____ and he knows he can save him, then he is obligated to do so. (19:16)

י If one wants to fear his parent, then he should not _____, and not _____, and not _____. (19:3)

כ Who is obligated to fear their mother and father? (19:3)

ל Why is the מצוה of שבת connected to the מצוה of fearing one's parent? (19:3)

מ What are some of the ways by which people respect their parents? (19:3)

נ The years of ערלה of a fruit tree begin from the time of _____. (19:23)

ס What kind of death does a person receive when the תורה uses the words דמיו בו, as it does by someone who curses his parents? (20:9)

ע An _____ describes the _____. (20:2)

פ Words describing the ends of the beard and its five marked areas. (19:27)

פ, צ שעטנז is clothing made of both _____ and _____. (19:19)

ק The words אשת איש teach us that a _____ cannot fulfill _____. (20:10)

ר The פרשה of קדושים was offered in הקהל because _____. (19:1)

ש The אבני צדק are stones _____. (19:36)

ת Perverting judgment is a _____. (19:15)

קדושים

Answers

א. אין בנין בית המקדש דוחה שבת

the construction of the Beit Hamikdash does not override the Shabbat

ב. בין הבהמה הטהרה לטמאה, בין טהורה לך לטמאה לך, בין שנשחט רבו של סימן לנשחט לנשחט חציו

between a pure and impure animal, between that [animal] which is pure to you and impure to you, between that [animal] whose signs were mostly slaughtered and [an animal] whose signs were only slaughtered halfway

ג. גלה, גלוי

exposed, exposure

ד. דעו את מי אתם מחליפין את מי

Know Who you are exchanging for whom

ה. הוו פרושים מן העריות ומן העבירה

Separate yourselves from promiscuous relationships and from sin

ו, ז. והתקדשתם, זו פרישות עבודה זרה

make yourselves holy, this [refers to] separation from idolatry

ח. חנק

strangulation

ט. טובע בנהר

drowning in a river

י. ישב במקומו, ידבר במקומו, יסתור את דבריו

[do not] sit in his place, [do not] speak in his place, [do not] contradict his words

כ. כל אחד מכם תיראו אביו ואמו

Every single one of you shall fear your mother and father.

ל. לומר אף על פי שהזהרתיך על מורא אב אם יאמר לך חלל את השבת אל
תשמע לו וכן בשאר כל המצות

*To tell [us]: even though you are warned to fear your father if he [your father] tells
you to desecrate the Shabbat you should not listen to him and so too with regard
to the other commandments.*

מ. מאכיל, משקה, מלביש, מנעיל, מכניס, מוציא

*feeding [him], providing [him] with drink, clothing [him], providing [him] with
shoes, escorting [him] in, escorting [him] out*

נ. נטיעתו

planting

ס. סקילה

stoning

ע. עם הארץ, עם שעתידין לירש את הארץ על ידי מצות הללו

*nation of the land, nation who will in the future inherit the land by [adhering to]
these commandments*

פ. פאת זקנך

corners of the beard

פ, צ. צמר, פשתים

wool, flax

ק. קטן, קידושין

minor, marriage

ר. רוב גופי התורה תלויין בה

the majority of the essentials of the Torah depend upon it

ש. ששוקלין כנגדן

against which [things] are weighed

ת. תועבה

despicable act

Questions

ב, א The words _____ include _____ in becoming טמא through contact with the dead, and exclude _____, who are allowed to become טמא.(21:1)

ג Which word describes a break-out rash? (22:22)

ה, ד Someone who ate _____ by mistake has to give the כהן _____, like fruits that will become _____, to replace that which was eaten. (22:14)

ו, ה When the תורה instructs, "_____" about ראש השנה, it is referring to _____. (23:25)

ז The first oil which comes out of the _____ is called "_____." (24:2)

ח Why was a כבש brought with the קרבן העומר? (23:12)

ט The תורה refers to the מנורה as _____, which means that the gold it was made out of had to be _____ or that before it was used it had to be _____, cleaned from its ashes. (24:4)

י The word _____ teaches that only an animal that is born naturally cannot be offered as a קרבן for the first seven days; however, an animal which is _____ can be offered right away. (22:27)

כ The מקלל was stoned by _____. The word _____ comes to include the judges and the expression _____ means in front of the entire assembly. (24:14)

ל Why does the תורה instruct the כהנים explicitly, _____, repeating the word "scratch"? (21:5)

נ, מ A זונה is a woman who _____, such as a _____ or a _____, and a חללה is a woman who _____, such as the daughter of a widow who married a כהן גדול. (21:7)

ס, ע The _____ that ה' sat בני ישראל in were _____. (23:43)

ע, פ An אתרוג is called _____, which means that it is an _____. (23:40)

פ What is a כהן גדול forbidden to grow on his head for more than thirty days? (21:10)

צ Which words in the תורה introduce the מצוה of the candles? (24:2)

ק, ר The תורה commands with regard to each כהן, "_____," which means he should be treated with _____; for example, he should be_____, such as _____. (21:8)

ש Which word in the פרשה refers to a Kohen's wife? (21:2)

ת A type of instrument which is אסור to use for shaving because it destroys. (21:5)

Answers

א, ב. בני אהרן, אף בעלי מומין, בנות אהרן
sons of Aharon, even those with a blemish, daughters of Aharon

ג. גרב
break-out rash

ד, ה. הקדש, דבר הראוי להיות קדש, הקדש
sanctified item, something that is worthy of being sanctified, sanctified item

ה, ו. והקרבתם אשה, המוספים האמורין בחומש הפקודים
and you shall sacrifice a fire offering, the Musaf sacrifices that are mentioned in Bamidbar

ז. זית, זך
olive, clear

ח. חובה לעומר הוא בה
It comes as an obligation for the Omer

ט. טהורה, טהור, טהרה
pure, pure, purified

י. יולד, יוצא דופן
born, exits the womb

כ. כל העדה, כל, כל העדה
the entire congregation, all, the entire congregation

ל. לא ישרטו שרטת, לחיב על כל שריטה ושריטה
do not scratch scratches, to make one liable for each and every scratch

מ, נ. נבעלה בעילת ישראל האסור לה, נתין, ממזר, נולדה מן הפסולים שבכהנה
[a woman] who has had relations with a person who is forbidden to her, natin, mamzer, someone who was born from a relationship forbidden for Kohanim

ס, ע. סכת, ענני הכבוד

huts, clouds of glory

ע, פ. פרי עץ הדר, עץ שטעם עצו ופריו שוה

fruit of a beautiful tree, a tree whose bark and fruit taste the same

פ. פרע על האבל

long hair for a state of mourning

צ. צו את בני ישראל

"Command to Bnei Yisrael"

ק, ר. קדוש יהיה לך, קדושה, ראשון בכל דבר, ראשון לברך בסעודה

he shall be holy for you, holiness, first privilege in all services, first to lead the blessings on a meal

ש. שארו

relative

ת. תער

razor blade

בהר

Questions

א One is not allowed to prostrate oneself on an _____, _____, because _____. (26:1)

ב בני ישראל are privileged to receive ארץ ישראל "_____." (25:38)

ב, ג A _____ is obligated _____. (25:54)

ד What is the only circumstance under which a person is allowed to sell his field? (25:25)

ה What type of state is the land supposed to be in during the year of שמיטה? (25:5)

ו Which word teaches us that one has to sanctify the יובל year at its onset in the בית דין? (25:10)

ז What does the תורה refer to when it instructs people not to victimize one another in financial sales? (25:14)

ח Even though all of the מצות were said at סיני, _____. (25:2)

ט Another word for "cities." (25:31)

י The word _____ always refers to _____. (25:29)

כ What is someone who leaves ארץ ישראל compared to? (25:38)

ל The שמיטה year is a year of rest _____, _____ and _____. (25:4)

ל, מ The word _____ is a _____. (26:1)

נ On the יובל year even a servant who was _____ goes free. (25:10)

ס What inevitably happens on יובל year to land which was purchased before יובל? (25:15)

ע Even if a person cannot pay his debts and becomes an _____, one should not make such a person perform _____, which is _____. (25:39)

בהר

פ, צ The land of ארץ ישראל can never be sold _____, which means _____, for an everlasting sale, (25:23)

ק What happens when שמיטה is followed by יובל? (25:11)

ר Someone who sold or relinquished ownership of his field is not _____ because it has to belong to the new owner for at least two years. (25:15)

ש What is the proper way that one should treat his servants during the שמיטה year? (25:6)

ת When selling a portion of land, one must assess its value according to the number of years left until יובל. If there are many years left until the יובל, then _____, which means _____, and if there are fewer years left until the יובל, then _____, which means _____. (25:16)

בהר

Answers

א. אבן משכית, אפילו לשמים, אסרה תורה לעשות כן חוץ מן המקדש

flooring stone, even for the sake of Heaven, the Torah forbade one from doing so outside of the Mikdash

ב. בשכר שתקבלו מצוותי

[as] reward for your accepting My commandments

ב, ג. גוי, במזונות בניו

non-Jew, in providing food for his children

ד. דוחק עוני

hard-pressed poverty

ה. הפקר יהיה הכל

[It shall be] free for all to take

ו. וקדשתם

and you shall sanctify

ז. זו אונאת ממון

This [refers to] victimizing someone financially

ח. חזרו ונשנו בערבות מואב

They reviewed and learned them over again at the Plains of Moav

ט. טירתם

cities

י. ימים, ימי שנה שלימה

days, the days of a full year

כ. כעובד עבודה זרה

[He is] like someone who worships idolatry

ל. לארץ, לשדות, לכרמים

for the land, for the fields, for the vineyards

ל, מ. משכית, לשון כיסוי

flooring, language referring to a cover

נ. נרצע

pierced [to indicate continued slavery]

ס. סופו לההחזירה לו בשנת היובל

In the end the land will return to him at the Yovel (Jubilee) year.

ע. עבד עברי, עבודת עבד, עבודה של גנאי

indentured Jewish servant, a servant's work, degrading work

פ, צ. צמתת, פסיקה

forever, severed

ק. קדושות סמוכות זו לזו

Two holy [years] next to one another

ר. רשאי לגאול פחות משתי שנים

[not] permitted to redeem it within fewer than two years

ש. שלא תנהוג בהם כבעל הבית

[That he] should not treat them as an owner [normally would].

ת. תרבה מקנתו, תמכרנה ביוקר, תמעיט מקנתו, תמעיט בדמיה

increase the purchase, sell it at high price, decrease the purchase, reduce the price

בחקותי

Questions

א What did 'ה say He will do in order to reward בני ישראל? (26:9)

א, ב One of the _____ that 'ה will grant בני ישראל regarding food is, "_____." (26:5)

ב, ג If בני ישראל keep the מצות, then 'ה promises to grant _____, which means that the rain will fall _____, such as _____. (26:4)

ד A type of produce from which one is obligated to give מעשר. (27:30)

ה, ו The words _____ teach us "_____," and that we should learn תורה for the sake of fulfilling its commandments, as it says, "_____." (26:3)

ז What does the משכן refer to? (26:11)

ח, ט A _____ animal is an animal with a blemish, which means it is therefore _____; the only way that קדשים can become _____ and be redeemed is when they are blemished. (27:11)

י The תורה describes someone who is _____ a vow; this means he is _____ to express the vow. (27:2)

כ What did 'ה want בני ישראל to understand when He reminded them, אני יהוה אלהיכם? (26:13)

ל If בני ישראל _____ to 'ה, which means they would not be interested _____, then they will be cursed. (26:14)

מ 'ה promised בני ישראל that their enemies would flee _____. (26:8)

נ Why is one instructed to hit the tenth animal with a stick in order to separate it? (27:32)

ס There is an argument regarding property that a person separates for 'ה; some are of the opinion that _____ belong to הקדש, and some are of the opinion that _____ belong to the כהנים. (27:28)

ע The _____ are regular trees that are blessed to _____. (26:4)

פ When a person does _____, he is required to add on a fifth of the value. (27:13)

צ A person uses a staff _____ to separate the animals designated for מעשר. (27:32)

ק How will בני ישראל stand as they increase in numbers? (26:9)

ר _____ means that בני ישראל will become frightful with softness of the heart. (26:36)

ש ה׳ promised _____ to בני ישראל; _____ – from this we learn _____. (26:6)

ת One is not allowed to exchange a _____ once he has designated the animal for a קרבן. (27:10)

בחקותי

Answers

א. אפנה מכל עסקי לשלם שכרכם

[I] will turn away from all My concerns in order to grant you "reward".

א, ב. ברכות, אוכל קמעא והוא מתברך במעיו

blessings, [you] will eat little bits and it will be blessed in your insides [to feel satisfied]

ב, ג. גשמים בעתם, בשעה שאין דרך בני אדם לצאת, בלילי שבת

rain in its proper time, at a time when people normally do not go outside, Friday nights

ד. דגן

grain

ה, ו. ואת מצותי תשמרו, הוו עמלים בתורה, ולמדתם אתם ושמרתם לעשתם

"and you shall keep My commandments," labor over [study of] Torah, and you shall learn them and you shall observe them in order to perform them

ז. זה בית המקדש

This is the Beit Hamikdash

ח, ט. טמא, טמאה להקרבה, חולין

impure, impure [unfit] for sacrifice, mundane

י. יפליא, יפרש בפיו

express, expresses openly with his mouth

כ. כדאי אני שתאמינו בי שאני יכול לעשות כל אלה

I am worthy that you should believe in Me because of all [the miracles] I can do.

ל. לא תשמעו, ליהיות עמלים בתורה

do not listen, to labor over the [study of] Torah

מ. מן החלשים שבכם ולא מן הגבורים שבכם

from the weak amongst you and not from the mighty amongst you

נ. ניכר שהוא מעשר

[So that] it is recognizable that it is [part of] Maaser

ס. סתם חרמים, סתם חרמים

unspecified vows, unspecified vows

ע. עץ השדה, עתידין לעשות פירות

tree of the field, bear fruit in the future

פ. פדיון מעשר שני

redeeming of the Maaser Sheini

צ. צבוע בסיקרא

colored with red coloring

ק. קומה זקופה

Straight and erect

ר. רך לבב

softness of the heart

ש. שלום, שמא תאמרו הרי מאכל והרי משתה אם אין שלום אין כלום, שהשלום שקול כנגד הכל

peace, perhaps you will say [that] "we have what to eat and drink" – but if there is no peace then all is for naught, that peace is the equivalent of having everything

ת. תם בבעל מום

whole animal [in exchange for] a blemished animal

במדבר

Bamidbar

Questions

א When the תורה says _____ it is referring to _____. (1:17)

ב, ג Every male over twenty was counted by using a _____ per every _____. (1:2)

ד The מחתת would collect the _____. (4:9)

ה, ו When the תורה says _____, it means that _____ in order to trace the ancestry of each person to his שבט. (1:18)

ז אהרן and the כהנים were charged with guarding the מקדש to ensure that a _____ would not approach it. (3:6)

ח What happens to people who touch the קדש? (4:15)

ט What do we learn from the fact that the three שבטים who camped closest to משה became great תורה scholars? (3:38)

י Which word means that a person will be put to death by the hand of ה'? (1:51)

כ List the three times when ה' counted בני ישראל. (1:1)

ל The tribe of _____ was considered the _____ and therefore was worthy _____. (1:49)

מ A _____ refers to any _____ to which a man is _____ and of which it is _____, to fulfill his duty. This is the case in any _____ or in any _____ in which the word appears. (3:7)

מ, נ The כהנים removed the ashes in order to clean the _____. (4:16)

נ What is on top of the word ואהרן and why? (3:39)

ס Once a child reaches one month old he can no longer be considered a _____. (3:40)

ע What was one of the important jobs that אלעזר was in charge of? (4:16)

פ The words ואת אהרן ואת בניו תפקד refers to _____, which is to be appointed. (3:10)

צ Every שבט had its own flag with its own _____ and each _____ was like the color of the שבט's stone. (2:2)

ק ה' said that if בני ישראל perform the מצות, then there would be no _____ but if strangers try to take jobs that are not theirs, such as was the case with _____, then there would be _____. (1:53)

ר After a cloth was spread over the מזבח, where did the fire that descended from the Heavens rest on the מזבח? (4:13)

ש What do we learn from the words "כל יצא צבא"? (1:3)

ת What did the כהנים do when they saw the cloud starting to disperse? (2:9)

Answers

א. את האנשים האלה, את שנים עשר נשיאים הללו

these designated men, these designated twelve princes

ב, ג. בקע, גלגלת

half shekel (coin), head

ד. דשן הנרות כשמטיבן

the ashes of the candles as they are prepared [for lighting]

ה, ו. ויתילדו על משפחתם, הביאו ספרי יחוסיהם

established their genealogy according to their families, they brought the books of their descent

ז. זר

stranger

ח. חיבין מיתה בידי שמים

They are liable to death at the hands of Heaven

ט. טוב לצדיק טוב לשכנו

Good for the righteous person [and] good for his neighbor.

י. יומת

[he] will die.

כ. כשיצאו ממצרים, כשנפלו בעגל, כשבא להשרות שכינתו עליהם

when they came out of Mitzrayim, when they fell by the [golden] calf, when [Hashem] came to rest His Divine spirit upon them

ל. לוי, לגיון של מלך, להיות נמנה לבדו

Levi, chosen Legion of the king, to be counted by itself

מ. משמרת, מינוי, ממונה עליו, מטל עליו לעשותו, מקרא, משנה

guard group, appointment, appointed on [it], obligatory for him to do [his duty], written law, Mishna

מ, נ. מזבח נחשת

copper Mizbeach (Altar)

נ. נקוד על ואהרן לומר שלא היה במנין הלוים

There are dots over the word "and Aharon" to demonstrate that he was not included in the counting of the Leviim.

ס. ספק נפל

one who might be a nefel

ע. עליו מטל לצוות ולזרז ולהקריב בעת חניתן

He has the obligation to direct and encourage and offer sacrifices during the time that Bnei Yisrael camp.

פ. פקידות

appointing

צ. צבע, צבע

color, color

ק. קצף, קורח, קצף

anger, Korach, anger

ר. רבוצה תחת הבגד כארי בשעת המסעות

Crouched under the garment much like a lion [would crouch] at the time of journeys.

ש. שאין יוצא בצבא פחות מבן עשרים

[We learn] that one who is younger then twenty years of age does not go out as part of the army.

ת. תוקעין הכהנים בחצוצרות

The Kohanim would blow the trumpets.

נשא

Questions

א לבנה was not added to the קרבן סוטה because the סוטה did not exemplify the behavior of the _____ and our _____ are referred to as לבנה. (5:15)

ב, ג The כהן uncovers the hair of the סוטה because _____ is considered a _____ for _____. (5:18)

ד The encampment of בני ישראל was marked by _____. (5:2)

ה What does the תורה mean when it refers to the עבודה of the לוים? (4:47)

ו What served as the screen to the entrance of the אוהל מועד? (4:25)

ז Who is a man who has no redeemer? (5:8)

ח This word refers to the seeds of grapes. (6:4)

ט משה did not _____ from the construction of the משכן, which is why he was credited with completing it. (7:1)

י The word _____ means _____, which is to separate himself. (6:2)

כ What was the day on which the משכן was completed likened to? (7:1)

ל It was necessary to count the _____ in order _____. (4:22)

מ How was the process of הנפה performed? (5:25)

נ, ס The פרשה of _____ is connected to the פרשה of _____. Why? (6:2)

ע The panels of the משכן refer to the _____. The אוהל מועד refers to panels of _____, which were _____, and the covers of the אוהל מועד were made from _____. (4:25)

פ The _____ offered by the נשיאים had to be the exceptional _____ of its herd. (7:15)

צ Which word refers to covered wagons? (7:3)

ק The _____ that משה heard from above the כפרת was the same _____. (7:89)

ר When a husband experiences a _____, then he warns his wife not to be alone with another man. (5:14)

ש How many camps were there when בני ישראל camped? (5:2)

ת What did the כף אחת correspond to in the sacrifice of the נשיאים and why? (7:20)

Answers

א. אמהות, אמהות

Matriarchs, Matriarchs

ב, ג. גילוי הראש, גנאי, בנות ישראל

uncovering the head, disgrace, daughters [women] of Yisrael

ד. דגלים

flags

ה. הוא השיר במצלתים וכנורות

This is the song with cymbals and harps

ו. וילון המזרחי

the eastern curtain

ז. זה הגר שמת ואין לו יורשים

This refers to a convert who died and has no heirs.

ח. חרצנים

seeds of grapes

ט. טעה בתבנית אחת

[did not] err with a single pattern

י. יפליא, יפריש

set apart, separate

כ. ככלה הנכנסת לחופה

Like a bride who enters the hupa [canopy for marriage]

ל. לויים, לראות כמה יש שהגיעו לכלל עבודה

Leviim, to see how many there are who reached the age worthy to work [in the Mishkan]

מ. מוליך, מביא, מעלה, מוריד

moving [the offering] forward, bringing [it] back, raising [it] up, lowering [it] down.

נ, ס. נזיר, סוטה

Nazir, Sotah

   The Rabbis explain that from here we learn that one who sees a Sotah in a state of disgrace should become a Nazir and abstain from drinking wine.

ע. עשר התחתונות, עזים, עשויות לאהל עליו, עורות אילים מאדמים

ten lower ones, goat's hair, made to cover over like a tent, red colored ram skins

פ. פר אחד, פר

one cow, cow

צ. צבים

wagons

ק. קול, קול שנדבר עמו בסיני

voice, the voice that spoke with him at Sinai

ר. רוח קנאה

spirit of jealousy

ש. שלש מחנות היו שם בשעת חניתן

Three camps were there at the time that they encamped.

ת. תורה

Torah

   There is only one Torah that Hashem gave to Bnei Yisrael. To verify this, the Nasi offered only one ladle.

Questions

א אהרן lit the מנורה _____, which meant _____ – not on the branches of the מנורה _____. (8:2)

ב The מן was compared to a _____, which is a fine stone, like crystal. (11:7)

ג Who was the youngster who ran to משה to inform him that אלדד and מידד were prophesying? (11:27)

ד From משה's תפילה to ה', אל נא רפא נא לה, we learn the concept of _____, that someone who asks _____ has to first say two or three _____ and then make his request. (12:13)

ה, ו The תורה uses the word _____ to demonstrate that _____ to משה how to make the מנורה. (8:4)

ז The people who were טמא and asked משה to bring a קרבן פסח were _____ to reveal the laws of פסח שני because we bring _____ by means of the _____. (9:7)

ח אהרן's reaction to the _____ was _____ because neither he nor the כהנים took part in the _____. ה' told אהרן, " _____." (8:2)

ט, י משה offered _____ a _____ in order to encourage him to join בני ישראל. (10:32)

י _____ was given his name because _____, which means that he caused more to be written in the תורה, as the advice he gave to משה was recorded. (10:29)

כ When would people come to ask משה and אהרן questions of הלכה? (9:6)

ל Why does it say בני ישראל five times in one passuk? (8:19)

מ What did אהרן and מרים mean when they referred to ציפורה as "האשה הכשית"? (12:1)

נ The cloud would fold up during the time that בני ישראל were
_____. (9:18)

ס, ע משה is described as an _____, which means he was a
_____. (12:3)

ע אהרן is instructed בהעלתך regarding the lighting of the מנורה
_____ because אהרן had to light the מנורה _____. In
addition, there was a step in front of the מנורה upon which the כהן
would _____. (8:2)

פ The _____ records the only _____ that בני ישראל offered
during their forty years in the desert. (9:1)

צ Which words demonstrate something that only 'ה could do and how?
(12:4)

ק משה was instructed, "_____," which means _____. (8:6)

ר What is another term that refers to those who hate בני ישראל? (10:35)

ש The מנורה had _____. These נרות were divided _____:
_____, and so, too, _____. What was the reason why? (8:2)

ת What happened to משה after בני ישראל complained to him that they
wanted meat? (11:15)

Answers

א. אל מול פני המנורה, אל מול נר האמצעי, אלא בגוף של מנורה

toward the face of the Menorah, toward the face of the middle candle, rather on the body of the Menorah

ב. בדלח

a fine stone

ג. גרשם בן משה

Gershom the son of Moshe

ד. דרך ארץ, דבר מחברו, דברי תחנונים

Derech Eretz [way of the land], something from his friend, words of supplication

ה, ו. וזה, הראהו הקדוש ברוך הוא באצבע לפי שנתקשה בה

"and this," Hashem showed [Moshe] with His finger [how to make the Menorah] because it was difficult [for Moshe] to do

ז. זוכה, זכות, זכאי

worthy, merit, worthy one(s)

ח. חנוכת הנשיאים, חלשה דעתו, חנוכה, חייך שלך גדולה משלהם שאתה מדליק ומטיב את הנרות

dedications of the princes, became upset, dedication, by your life! Your portion is far greater then theirs because you can light and prepare the candles

ט, י. יתרו, טובה

Yitro, favor

י. יתרו, יתר פרשה אחת בתורה

Yitro, [he caused] one extra portion to be included in the Torah

כ. כששניהם יושבין בבית המדרש באו ושאלום

When both of them would sit in the Beit Midrash people would come and ask them.

ל. להודיע חבתן

To demonstrate their endearment [to Hashem]

מ. מגיד שהכל מודים ביפיה

[This was] saying that all admitted to her beauty.

נ. נוסעים

traveling

ס, ע. ענו, סבלן

humble, tolerant

ע. על שם שהלהב עולה, עד שתהא השלהבת עולה מאליה, עומד ומטיב

Because of the fact that the flame rises, until the flame rises on its own, [he] stood and prepared

פ. פרשה, פסח

Parsha, Passover [sacrifice]

צ. צאו שלשתכם

you three go out
Hashem summoned Moshe, Aharon and Miriam; all three names in a single utterance.

ק. קח את הלויים, קחם בדברים

take the Leviim, take them with words

ר. רודפים

those who pursue

ש. שבעה נרות, ששה שעל ששת הקנים, שלשה המזרחיים פונים למול האמצעי, שלשה המערביים . . . למול האמצעי, שלא יאמרו לאורה הוא צריך

seven candles, six on the six branches, the three eastward candles faced the middle one, the three westward [candles] faced the middle one, so that no one can say that He needs the light

ת. תשש כחו של משה

Moshe's strength weakened.

Questions

א What was משה asking the מרגלים to check for when he told them to check if there is a tree in ארץ כנען? (13:20)

א, ב The מרגלים said that כנען was _____, meaning, "_____." (13:32)

ג The מרגלים described the כנענים as _____ and _____. (13:32)

ד What does the color of תכלת look like? (15:38)

ה, ו The words _____ mean that כלב _____. (13:30)

ז What did משה warn all of בני ישראל to discourage them from trying to conquer כנען right after the מרגלים were killed? (14:41)

ח Where was סקילה carried out? (15:36)

ט The punishment for those who were slanderous about ארץ ישראל was that their tongues stretched down to _____ and worms came out of their tongues and went into _____. (14:37)

י משה prayed for _____ saying, "_____." (13:16)

כ What do we learn from the fact that the מרגלים began their description of כנען as זבת חלב ודבש? (13:27)

ל, מ בני ישראל placed the _____ under imprisonment because they knew that _____, but _____. (15:34)

נ How does Hashem describe the pleasant fragrance from the קרבנות? (15:3)

ס What did משה provide for the מרגלים when he encouraged them to check if the people who dwelled in כנען were strong or weak? (13:18)

ע Who are the נפילים? (13:33)

פ משה did not want ה' to kill בני ישראל _____. (14:15)

צ יהושע told בני ישראל that the כנענים no longer have _____, which means that _____. (14:9)

ק, ר בני ישראל were instructed, "_____," to offer "_____" from the dough that they were _____. (15:20)

ש An example of a time when all בני ישראל have to offer a קרבן to atone for their mistake is if _____. (15:24)

ת This word means removal and describes how בני ישראל removed their hearts from (following) ה'. (14:34)

Answers

א. אם יש בהם אדם כשר שיגן עליהם בזכותו

If there is a decent man [among] them in whose merit they would be protected.

א, ב. ארץ אכלת יושביה, בכל מקום שעברנו מצאנום קוברי מתים

A land that devours its inhabitants, everywhere we went we found [they were] burying the dead

ג. גדולים, גבוהים

large, tall

ד. דומה לרקיע המשחיר לעת ערב

[It] resembles the sky as it gets darker toward the evening.

ה, ו. ויהס כלב, השתיק את כלם

Kalev hushed, he made everyone quiet

ז. זו שאתם עושים לא תצלח

This [plan] you are trying to do will not succeed.

ח. חוץ ורחוק מבית דין

Outside and far from Beit Din

ט. טבורם, טבורם

their navels, their navels

י. יהושע, יה יושיעך מעצת מרגלים

Yehoshua, G-d should save you from the devious plot of the spies

כ. כל דבר שקר שאין אומרים בו קצת אמת בתחלתו אין מתקיים בסופו

Any false statements which do not begin by including some truth are bound not to last.

ל, מ. מקשש עצים, מחלל שבת במיתה, לא היו יודעים באיזו מיתה ימות

gatherer of wood, [one who] desecrates Shabbat is subject to the death penalty, they were not sure which death penalty to impose on him

נ. נחת רוח לפני

pleasantness for Me

ס. סימן מסר להם

He provided them with a sign.

ע. ענקים מבני שמחזאי ועזאל שנפלו מן השמים בימי דור אנוש

Giants who were sons of Shamchazi and Azael who fell from the heavens during the generation of Enosh.

פ. פתאום

suddenly

צ. צלם, צלו של המקום סר מעליהם

protection, the shade of Hashem was removed from them

ק, ר. קדם שתאבלו, ראשית ערסתכם, רגילין ללוש במדבר

before you eat, beginnings of your kneadings, accustomed to knead in the desert

ש. ששגגו והורו על אחת מן העבודות שהיא מתרת לעבוד עבודה זרה בכך

that they mistakenly taught that it is permissible to worship idolatry in a particular way

ת. תנואה

removal

קרח

Questions

א, ב דתן and אבירם got involved with קרח _____, and from this we learn the concept _____. (16:1)

ג The לוים were also instructed, _____, to offer תרומת מעשר. (18:28)

ד, ה What did קרח mean when he complained רב לכם against משה (16:3), and what did משה mean when he responded to קרח, saying, רב לכם בני לוי? (16:7)

ו What were משה's four reactions to the four major sins of בני ישראל? (16:4)

ז, ח, ט תרומת מעשר, which the לוי gives to the כהן, is forbidden for _____ and _____ to eat; if they do eat it, then _____. (8:27)

ט What are פחים? (17:3)

י משה refers to ה' as אל אלהי הרוחות, which means _____. (16:22)

כ What are מחתות? (16:6)

ל ויקח קרח teaches us that קרח _____ in order _____ and _____. (16:1)

מ Which principal do we learn from the fact that משה pursued דתן and אבירם and summoned them in front of him? (16:12)

מ, נ, ס One can ask, _____? One answer provided is _____, and then קרח began his rebellion by rounding up 250 heads of the _____ to challenge משה. (16:1)

ע ה' expected the כהנים to warn all strangers from touching קדש. Therefore ה' told the כהנים, "_____." (18:1)

פ אהרן's staff sprouted forth with almonds because almonds are a _____ and so, too, someone who objects regarding the leadership of the כהנים, _____. (17:21)

פ, צ A _____ grew out of אהרן's staff, which is the emergence of a _____ after the _____. (17:23)

ק, ר The מלאך המות revealed to משה a _____ that the _____. (17:11)

ש Even though אהרן was a כהן, his name was inscribed on the staff of _____ to demonstrate that the כהנים and לוים were _____. (17:18)

ת The difference between the word _____ and _____ is that _____ refers to one complaint whereas _____ refers to many _____ even though it is written in singular form. (17:25)

Answers

א, ב. בשביל שהיה שבט ראובן שרוי בחניתם תימנה שכן לקהת ובניו החונים תימנה, אוי לרשע ואוי לשכנו

because the Tribe of Reuven rested and camped in the South direction as did their neighbors Kehat and his sons who also encamped in the South, woe to the wicked and woe to his neighbor[s]

ג. גם אתם תרימו ממעשר שלכם

you too are required to set aside from your tithe

ד, ה. הרבה יותר מדאי לקחתם לעצמכם גדלה, דבר גדול נטלתם בעצמכם לחלוק על הקדוש ברוך הוא

you have taken far too much prominence for yourselves, this was a huge undertaking you took upon yourselves to argue with Hakadosh Baruch Hu

ו. ויפל על פניו, ויחל משה, ויתפלל משה, ויאמר משה אל ה׳ ושמעו מצרים

[he] fell on his face, [he] pleaded, [he] prayed, [he] said to Hashem, "Egypt will hear"

ז, ח, ט. זרים, טמאים, חיבין עליה מיתה

strangers (non-Kohanim), the impure, [they are] subject to the death penalty

ט. טסים מרדדין

thinned out sheets

י. יודע מחשבות

[He] knows [people's] thoughts

כ. כלים שחותין בהם גחלים

utensils used to rake off coals

ל. לקח את עצמו לצד אחד, להיות נחלק מתוך העדה, לעורר על הכהנה

he took himself to one side, to separate [himself] from the congregation, to incite objections regarding the priesthood

מ. מכאן שאין מחזיקין במחלוקת

From here [we learn] that one should not encourage and maintain dispute.

מ, נ, ס. מה ראה קרח לחלוק עם משה, נתקנא על נשיאותו של אליצפן בן
עזיאל שמנהו משה נשיא על בני קהת, סנהדרין

*What did Korach see [that made him want] to differ with Moshe, [he] was jealous
regarding Moshe's appointment of Elytzafan ben Uziel as leader of children of
Kehath, Sanhedrin [high court of justice]*

ע. עליכם אני מטיל עונש הזרים

I place upon you the punishment of the strangers [non-Kohanim]

פ. פרי הממהר להפריח מכל הפרות, פורענותו ממהרת לבא

a fruit that blossoms fastest of all fruits, his punishment will come hastily

פ, צ. ציץ, פרי, פרח נופל

bud, fruit, flower falls

ק, ר. רז, קטרת עוצר המגפה

secret, the incense stops a plague

ש. שבט לוי, שבט אחד הוא

Tribe of Levi, was one Tribe

ת. תלונותם, תלונתם, תלונותם, תלונתם, תלונות

*their complaints, their complaints [spelled without a vav], their complaints, their
complaints [without a vav], complaints*

חקת

Questions

א What did משה mean when he promised the king of אדום that דרך המלך נלך? (20:17)

ב משה was instructed to remove אהרן's _____ and to place them on _____. (20:26)

ג ה' called the פרשה of פרה אדמה a חק because He wanted בני ישראל to understand that _____. (19:2)

ג, ד _____ is a type of _____, which the Egyptians died from. (20:3)

ה What did ה' say would have happened had משה and אהרן spoke to the rock instead of hitting it? (20:12)

ו Which words demonstrate that even though it was difficult for משה to bring Aharon to the place where he would expire, nonetheless he did not delay to fulfill ה's instructions? (20:26)

ז What does the word נפש refer to with regard to impurity? (19:13)

ח Where did אלעזר הכהן take the פרה אדמה? (19:3)

ט Why did the spirit of בני ישראל become frustrated? (21:4)

י, כ בני ישראל were instructed to take a פרה אדמה because _____, so, too, _____. (19:22{2})

כ The תורה says that _____ arrived at הר ההר, which means _____. (20:22)

ל Why did משה and אהרן hit the rock twice? (20:11)

מ What do we learn from the fact that the תורה says, right after מרים died, that בני ישראל had no water? (20:2)

נ בני ישראל and משה were like one because a _____. (21:21)

ס What happened to בני ישראל in מצרים? (20:15)

ע In which direction did the כהן stand while he sprinkled the blood of the פרה אדמה? (19:4)

ע, פ _____ is referred to as the _____ because he was _____. (21:34)

צ Whose deaths atone for בני ישראל? (20:1)

ק Since the מן was absorbed into the organs of the body, _____. (21:5)

ר Two ways to refer to the "top of the crest." (21:20)

ש, ת The תורה says that the פרה אדמה had to be _____, which means _____. בני ישראל are also _____ and if they are blemished _____, then _____ and in a state of purity, they would return to _____. (19:2,(22))

Answers

א. אנו חוסמים את בהמתנו ולא יטו לכאן ולכאן לאכול

We muzzle our animals so they do not stray to the side and eat.

ב. בגדי כהנה גדולה, בנו בפניו

garments of the High Priest, on his son in his presence

ג. גזרה היא מלפני אין לך רשות להרהר אחריה

it is My decree and you have no right to question or challenge it

ג, ד. גוע, דבר

death, plague

ה. הייתי מקדש לעיני העדה ואומרם מה סלע זה שאינו מדבר ואינו שומע
מקים דבורו של מקום קל וחומר אנו

I would have been sanctified in front of the Congregation as they would have said, "This rock which does not speak or hear but fulfills the command of Hashem, certainly we [human beings must fulfill His commandments]."

ו. ויעש משה

Moshe did

ז. זו רביעית דם

This is a [particular measurement] of blood

ח. חוץ לשלש מחנות

outside the three camps

ט. טורח הדרך שהקשה להם

The difficulties of the journey which challenged them

י, כ. כשם שהם פרקו נזמי הזהב לעגל משלהם, יביאו זו לכפרה משלהם

just as they removed their gold rings [to create] their own Golden Calf, they will bring this for their atonement

כ. כל העדה, כלם שלמים ועומדים לכנס לארץ

all the congregation, all were complete and prepared to enter the land

ל. לפי שבראשונה לא הוציא אלא טיפין

Because at first [the rock] excreted only a few drops [of water].

מ. מכאן שכל ארבעים שנה היה להם הבאר בזכות מרים

From here we learn that the well stayed with them [Bnei Yisrael] all forty years because of the merits of Miriam.

נ. נשיא הדור הוא ככל הדור

the leader of the generation is likened to the entire generation itself

ס. סבלנו צרות רבות

We suffered many hardships

ע. עומד במזרחו של ירושלים

He stands in the east of Yerushalayim

ע, פ. עוג, פליט, פלט מן הרפאים

Og, fugitive, [he] fled from the Rephaim

צ. צדיקים

the righteous

ק. קראוהו קלוקל

[they] called it insubstantial

ר. ראש הפסגה, ריש רמתא

highest point, top of the height

ש, ת. תמימה, שתהא תמימה באדמימות שאם היו בה שתי שערות שחורות פסולה, תמימים, תבוא זו ותכפר עליהם, תמותם

complete, that it should be completely red for if it had two black hairs it is disqualified, complete and whole, let this [red cow] atone for them [Bnei Yisrael], their wholesomeness

Questions

א What was בלעם trying to prove to ה' by expanding upon the entire name of בלק? (22:10)

ב Which famous principal do we learn from the words of the מלאך to בלעם, לך עם האנשים? (22:35)

ג בלק took בלעם to a place that was _____ in order to curse בני ישראל. (23:14)

ד בלק sacrificed only a _____ for בלעם and his officers. (22:40)

ה This word demonstrates that בלעם was embarrassed and degraded by his mule. (22:29)

ו Which word means "to fear"? (22:3)

ז The Mule told בלעם that he hit him _____, which reminded בלעם not to start with a nation who celebrates the שלש רגלים every year. (22:28)

ח What are משכנתיך? (24:5)

ט בלעם complemented בני ישראל, saying that in the morning they immediately put on their _____. (23:24)

י, כ The ברכה _____ means that בני ישראל will _____. (24:9)

ל, מ ה' asked בלעם, "_____?" – not because He did not know, rather _____. (22:9)

נ בלעם compared בני ישראל to _____ because they would _____. (24:6)

ס, ע The two kings who were the protectors of מדין and מואב. (22:5)

פ בלק told בלעם to go to the top of the _____ because he knew that in the future _____. (23:14)

בלק

צ בלק's question to בלעם, מה דבר ה׳, was a type of _____ making fun of בלעם. (23:17)

ק This word means tent. (25:8)

ר What caused פנחס to react to the חילול ה׳ in front of him? (25:7)

ש How many bad character traits did בלעם have? (And name them.) (24:2)

ת בלעם described that ה׳ took בני ישראל out of מצרים like _____, which can refer to _____ and demonstrates _____. (23:22)

בלק

Answers

א. אף על פי שאיני חשוב בעיניך חשוב אני בעיני המלכים

Even though I am not important in your eyes I am important in the eyes of the kings.

ב. בדרך שאדם רוצה לילך בה מוליכין אותו

The path which one wishes to walk on is the path on which they take him.

ג. גבוה

high up

ד. דבר מועט

an insignificant portion

ה. התעללת

mocked

ו. ויגר

frightened

ז. זה שלש רגלים

these three times

ח. חניותיך

your encampments

ט. טלית

Tallit

י, כ. כרע שכב כארי, יתישבו בארצם

crouched and lay down like a lion, [they] will settle their land

ל, מ. מי האנשים האלה עמך, להטעותו בא

who are these men with you, to mislead [Bilaam into thinking that Hashem does not necessarily know everything and therefore that he could fool Hashem and curse Bnei Yisrael]

נ. נחלים נטיו, נארכו ונמשכו לנטות למרחוק

streams spread out, extend and expand to spread out afar

ס, ע. סיחון, עוג

Sichon, Og

פ. פסגה, פרצה להפרץ בישראל משם

peak, a rupture would result in Yisrael's [strength] from there

צ. צחוק

laughter

ק. קבה

tent

ר. ראה מעשה ונזכר הלכה

[He] saw the deed and was reminded of the law

ש. שלש: עין רעה, רוח גבוהה, נפש רחבה

Three: evil eye, conceited spirit, broad spirit

ת. תועפת ראם לו, תוקף רום וגובה שלו, תוקף רב

the intensity of His loftiness, the intensity of the loftiness and the height that is His, great strength

Questions

א Which type of מלאכה is prohibited on יום טוב? (28:18)

ב Why did the תורה delineate the lineage of זמרי? (25:14)

ג משה leaned both his hands on יהושע's head like a vessel that is full and _____. (27:23)

ד What was משה instructed to tell יהושע regarding בני ישראל? (27:19)

ה What did the מדינים do that demonstrated their extreme hatred for the Jewish people? (25:15)

ו The daughters of צלפחד wanted משה to understand that their father sinned _____, as he was not part of the group who complained to משה, _____. (27:3)

ז _____ was also called צוחר. (26:13)

ח Even though the families of the לוים were counted, _____. (26:58)

ט The sacrificial offering of the evening had to be offered to the east of the _____. (28:3)

י All those males over twenty who had a name of their father's tribe partook in the lottery for a portion of ארץ ישראל; _____ and _____. (26:55)

כ What was ה's covenant with פנחס compared to? (25:12)

ל Why did the תורה delineate the lineage of פנחס? (25:11)

מ, נ The _____ were _____, therefore they were not included in the decree of the _____. (26:64)

נ Why is the scent from the קרבנות described by ה' as a ריח ניחח? (28:8)

ס, ע יהושע stood in front of the entire _____, which refers to the _____. (27:20)

ע The eighth day of the סוכות Holiday is called _____ because בני ישראל would be _____. (29:35)

פ What is said regarding the faces of משה and יהושע, respectively? (27:20)

צ This word means to remember. (25:17)

ק, ר On _____ the כהן also offers _____ for _____. (29:6)

ש The _____ offered as sacrifices on סוכות corresponded to the _____ nations. (29:18)

ת What did the women say that demonstrated their love for ארץ ישראל? (26:64)

פנחס

Answers

א. אפילו מלאכה הצריכה לכם

Even work which is necessary for you

ב. במקום שיחס את הצדיק לשבח יחס את הרשע לגנאי

In the same place that [the Torah] delineates the lineage of the righteous for praise, it delineates the lineage of a wicked person for disparagement.

ג. גדוש

pouring over

ד. דע שטרחנין הם סרבנים הם

Know that they [Bnei Yisrael] are troublesome and they are obstinate.

ה. הפקירו בת מלך לזנות כדי להחטיא את ישראל

They set loose the daughter of a king to behave promiscuously in order to cause Yisrael to sin.

ו. ולא החטיא את אחרים עמו, ולא בעדת קרח שהצו על הקדוש ברוך הוא

[but he] did not cause others to sin with him, and he was not from the assembly of Korach who incited people against Hashem.

ז. זרח

Zerach

ח. חסר כאן משפחות השמעי והעזריאלי וקצת מן היצהרי

there is missing here the Shimite and Azrielite families and some of the members of the families of Yitzhar

ט. טבעות

rings

י. יצאו יהושע וכלב, יצאו גרים ועבדים

[this] excludes Yehoshua and Kalev, excludes converts and servants

כ. כאדם המחזיק טובה וחנות למי שעושה עמו טובה

[It was] likened to someone who attributes goodness and graciousness to someone who [in turn] was kind to him.

ל. לפי שהיו השבטים מבזים אותו

Because the tribes would humiliate him [by making insulting comments].

מ, נ. נשים, מחבבות את הארץ, מרגלים

women, [they] loved the land, spies

נ. נחת רוח לפני

[It] fills Me with pleasant spirit

ס, ע. עדה, סנהדרין

congregation, Sanhedrin [court]

ע. עצרת, עצורים בעשית מלאכה

restraining stop, restrained from performing work

פ. פני משה כחמה פני יהושע כלבנה

Moshe's countenance was likened to the sun; Yehoshua's countenance was likened to the moon.

צ. צרור

remember

ק, ר. ראש השנה, קרבנות מוסף, ראש חודש

Rosh Hashana, Musaf sacrifices, new month

ש. שבעים פרים, שבעים

seventy cows, seventy

ת. תנה לנו אחזה

Give us a portion

Questions

א What type of נדרים can a husband absolve his wife from without her consent? (30:14)

ב When the תורה says _____, it refers to _____. (30:11)

ג Which הלכות did משה forget as a result of his getting angry? (31:21)

ד What is a כומז? (31:50)

ה How does one commit a נדר? (30:3)

ו Two words which describe what 'ה did to בני ישראל in the desert. (32:13)

ז What are the כלי הקדש? (31:6)

ח Why did משה speak to the leaders of the שבטים prior to בני ישראל? (30:2)

ט, י, כ The rule with regard to purifying _____ that became _____ is _____, so if a _____ had been used for cooking in hot water, _____; and if a _____ had been used for roasting, _____. (31:23)

ל A נדר only counts _____ but not _____. (30:3)

מ, נ 'ה instructed _____ to take _____ on the _____, but not _____, because the _____ were afraid and _____, whereas the _____ were hostile and _____. (31:3)

ס, ע The territories which בני גד and בני ראובן wanted were from the lands of _____ and _____. (32:3)

פ The Torah says that Moshe sent a thousand men from each שבט and _____. This equation implies that _____. (31:5)

צ What type of people did משה have to amass for an army? (31:3)

ק There were two cities which were called _____. (32:8)

ר A father can annul his daughter's נדר as long as she is still is under his
_____, like a נערה (30:4.)

ש What do we learn from the words אותם ואת פנחס? (31:6)

ת What did בני גד and בני ראובן request from משה? (32:32)

Answers

א. אינו מפר אלא נדרי עינוי נפש בלבד

[He] can only annul vows of personal affliction.

ב. בית אישה נדרה, בנשואה הכתוב מדבר

[she] vowed in her husband's house, the verse refers to a married woman

ג. גיעולי גוים

cleansing vessels used by non-Jews [for cooking]

ד. דפוס של בית הרחם

a plate adorning the womb area

ה. האומר הרי עלי

One says, "I take upon myself . . ."

ו. וינעם, ויטלטלם

[He] made them wander, [He] moved them

ז. זה הארון והציץ

This is referring to the Aron and the Tzitz.

ח. חלק כבוד לנשיאים ללמדם תחילה

He showed respect to the leaders by teaching them first.

ט, י, כ. כלים, טמא, כדרך תשמישו, כלי, יגעילנו בחמין, כלי, ילבנו באור

utensils, impure, the normal way it is used, utensil, we immerse it in hot water, utensil, we make it white in fire

ל. לאסור את המותר, להתיר את האסור

to forbid the permissible, to permit the forbidden

מ, נ. משה, נקמה, מדינים, מאת המואבים, מואבים, נכנסו לדבר מחמת יראה, מדינים, נתעברו על ריב לא להם

Moshe, revenge, Midyanim, from the Moavim, Moavim, entered the issue out of fear, Midyanim, interfered with a dispute which did not involve them

מטות

ס, ע. סיחון, עוג

Sichon, Og

פ. פנחס בן אלעזר הכהן, פנחס שקול כנגד כלם

Pinchas the son of Elazar the Kohen, Pinchas was equal to all of them (in importance)

צ. צדיקים

righteous

ק. קדש

Kadesh

ר. רשות

authority

ש. שהיה פנחס שקול כנגד כלם

That Pinchas was equal to all of them [in importance].

ת. תהי אחזת נחלתנו מעבר הזה

Let our land portion be on this side [of the Jordan].

Questions

א, ב ה׳ said that He dwells _____, which means _____. (35:34)

ג ארץ ישראל was divided up by means of a _____. (34:2)

ג, ד If the _____ finds the murderer outside the _____ of a city of refuge and he kills him, the תורה says that the murderer has no _____ because he was already considered dead. (35:27)

ה, ו When the תורה instructs, "_____" with regard to the cities of refuge, it means _____, which is to prepare. (35:11)

ז בני ישראל were not allowed to _____ in the cities of the לוים. (35:2)

ח Which place was at the end of the Northern Boundary? (34:9)

ט The תורה demonstrates that the מצרים were still _____. (33:4)

י ארץ ישראל would be divided amongst the שבטים according to the numbers of the _____. (33:54)

כ A סנהדרין can function outside of ארץ ישראל _____. (35:29)

ל Part of the reason why the תורה recorded all of the travels of בני ישראל in the desert was _____. (33:1)

מ, נ _____ through a _____ from ה׳. (33:38)

ס The תורה describes the תצאת הגבול which are the _____. (34:8)

ע The _____ departed when אהרן died. (33:40)

פ How was the southern side of ארץ ישראל, running from east to west, referred to? (34:3)

צ בני ישראל had to provide the לוים with all _____. (35:3)

ק One of the _____, or edges, of ארץ ישראל is to the south of _____. (34:4)

ר This place received its name after the לשון הרע that the מרגלים spoke.

ש The _____ ran the distance of _____. (33:49)

ת ה׳ told בני ישראל that if they take the land from its inhabitants, then _____ in ארץ ישראל. (33:53)

Answers

א, ב. בתוך בני ישראל, אף בזמן שהם טמאים

within Bnei Yisrael, even at a time when they are impure

ג. גורל

lottery

ג, ד. גאל הדם, גבול, דם

avenger of the blood, boundary, blood

ה, ו. והקריתם, הזמנה

you shall arrange, preparation

ז. זורע זרע

sow seeds

ח. חצר עינן

Hatzar Einan

ט. טרודים באבלם

preoccupied with their mourning

י. יוצאי מצרים

[those who] came out of Egypt

כ. כל זמן שנוהגת בארץ ישראל

all the while that the institution functions in Eretz Yisrael as well

ל. להודיע חסדיו של מקום

to inform [us] of Hashem's kindness

מ, נ. משה מת, נשיקה

Moshe died, kiss

ס. סופי הגבול

ends of the boundaries

ע. ענני הכבוד

clouds of glory

פ. פאת נגב

corner of the south

צ. צרכיהם

their needs

ק. קצות, קדש ברנע

edges, Kadesh Barnea

ר. רתמה

Ritma

ש. שיעור מחנה ישראל, שנים עשר מיל

dimensions of the camp of Yisrael, twelve mils

ת. תוכלו להתקים בה

[they will] be able to last there

דברים
Devarim

Questions

א Which title refers to צדיקים? (1:13)

ב _____ refers to the three places where _____ sinned, which were _____, _____ and _____. (1:1)

ג The תורה says that the מרגלים came down from ארץ ישראל to בני ישראל. From here we learn that ארץ ישראל is _____. (1:25)

ד, ה משה refers to a place called _____, which received its name because משה _____. (1:1)

ה What do we know about ראובן and גד with regard to fighting our enemies? (3:18)

ו The תורה warns, regarding the children of עשו, "_____," which means that we should not provoke them. (2:4)

ז, ח ה׳ said that no one would receive the land they walked on _____, who would inherit _____. (1:36)

ט When משה despairs saying that he cannot deal with בני ישראל's _____ he demonstrated that בני ישראל were _____. (1:12)

י The ברכה _____ was from משה to בני ישראל, but משה assured בני ישראל that ה׳ _____. (1:11)

כ What are men who are חכמים described as? (1:13)

ל סיחון attacked בני ישראל, which teaches us that _____ and _____. (2:32)

מ Where is the כנרת? (3:17)

מ, נ _____ are wise people whose wisdom is distinguished by the fact that they _____. (1:13)

ס משה learned from ה׳'s offering the תורה to various nations first in _____ that he, too, should first offer _____ peace before he confronted him in battle.

ע _____ miraculously on the day when בני ישראל battled
_____. (2:25)

פ _____ are cities that are _____. (3:5)

צ Which area, in the travels of בני ישראל in the desert, was all uphill?
(3:1)

ק What did משה mean when he compared בני ישראל to כוכבי השמים
לרב? (1:10)

ר What type of men was משה instructed to collect to assist him? (1:13)

ש, ת There is no actual place _____; rather it was called
_____, _____. (1:1)

Answers

א. אנשים

men

ב. בערבה, בני ישראל, בבעל פעור, בשטים, בערבות מואב

in the plain, Bnei Yisrael, [by] Baal Peor, [by] Shittim, [by] the Plains of Moav

ג. גבוהה מכל הארצות

higher then all of the lands

ד, ה. די זהב, הוכיחן על העגל שעשו בשביל רוב זהב שהיה להם

Di Zahav, reprimanded them regarding the Golden Calf that they made out of the large amount of gold that they had

ה. הם היו הולכים לפני ישראל למלחמה לפי שהיו גבורים

They would walk in front of Yisrael and lead them out to war because they were strongest.

ו. ונשמרתם מאד

and you shall take great care

ז, ח. זולתי כלב בן יפנה, חברון

except for Kalev Ben Yefuneh, Hevron

ט. טרחכם, טרחנין

your[plural] trouble, troublesome

י. יסף עליכם ככם אלף פעמים, יברך אתכם כאשר דבר לכם

[Hashem will] add to you a thousand times like you, He will bless you as He told you [He would]

כ. כסופים

revered

ל. לא שלח בשביל עוג לעזור לו, ללמדך שלא היו צריכים זה לזה

he did not send for Og to help him, [this] teaches that they were not in need of one another

מ. מעבר הירדן המזרחי היה

It was from the eastern side of the Jordan.

מ, נ. נבנים, מבינים דבר מתוך דבר

wise, wisely understand the meaning of one issue from within another

ס. סיני, סיחון

Sinai, Sichon

ע. עמדה חמה למשה, עוג

the sun stood still for Moshe, Og

פ. פרוזות, פתוחות בלא חומה

unenclosed [cities], open without a [surrounding] wall

צ. צד צפון

[The] northern side.

ק. קימים לעולם כחמה וכלבנה וככוכבים

[That they too are] lasting eternally like the sun, moon and stars

ר. ראשים ומכבדים עליכם

Leaders and dignitaries over [the people.]

ש, ת. ששמו תפל ולבן, תפל, שתפלו על המן שהוא לבן

Whose name was Tofel and Lavan, Tofel, [since they] besmirched the Man which was white

ואתחנן

Questions

א, ב The תורה says _____, which means that one must be devoted to 'ה _____. (6:5)

ג This word refers to the goodness of 'ה. (3:24)

ד After he conquered the lands of סיחון and עוג, משה said to 'ה, "_____," and he could enter ארץ ישראל. (3:23)

ה, ו Which types of laws does the תורה contain? (4:8)

ו משה instructed בני ישראל _____, which refers to the obligation to learn תורה. (4:6)

ז What is ואתחנן? (3:23)

ח The תורה prohibits one from adding on to a מצוה; for example, one should not have _____ or _____ or _____. (4:2)

ח, ט The תורה describes ארץ ישראל as a place where wells are _____ because it is a country full of _____. (6:12)

י What does the הר הטוב refer to? (3:25)

כ Why does the תורה say that 'ה's voice did not stop? (5:19)

ל The prohibition _____ means _____, which forbids a person _____. (7:2)

מ One is required to place one _____ on every doorway. (6:9)

נ A word which is used to describe a request. (3:25)

ס It is prohibited to form even the _____ or form of an idol. (4:16)

ע משה warned יהושע _____ and _____ and _____. (3:28)

פ How did משה prepare himself to stand in front of 'ה? (3:24)

פ, צ בני ישראל were instructed to destroy the _____ and _____ of foreign nations. (7:5)

ק When did 'ה command בני ישראל to keep שבת? (5:12)

ר What did משה express about 'ה when he referred to Him as אדני אלוהים? (3:24)

ש One has to put a מזוזה even on the posts of _____, _____, and _____. (6:9)

ש, ת The sign one wears on one's arm is the _____ and the sign between one's eyes is the _____. (6:8)

Answers

א, ב. בכל מאדך, אפילו הוא נוטל את נפשך
with all of your resources, even if He takes your soul

ג. גדלך
Your greatness

ד. דמיתי שמא התר הנדר
I thought perhaps the vow was annulled

ה, ו. הגונים ומקבלים
fair and acceptable

ו. ושמרתם
and you shall guard [them]

ז. זה אחד מעשרה לשונות שנקראת תפילה
This is one of the ten usages that refer to prayer.

ח. חמש פרשיות בתפלין, חמשת מינין בלולב, חמש ציציות
five passages in the Tefillin, five species for the myrtle, five Tzitziyot

ח, ט. חצובים, טרשין וסלעים
hewn out, stony ground and rocks

י. ירושלים
Yerushalayim

כ. כי קולו חזק וקים לעולם
Because His voice is strong and eternal.

ל. לא תחנם, לא תתן להם חן, לומר כמה נאה גוי זה
do not consider them favorably, do not offer them favor, to say "how beautiful is that nation"

מ. מזוזה
mezuzah

נ. נא

request

ס. סמל

symbol

ע. על הטרחות, על המשאות, על המריבות
regarding the troubles, regarding the burdens, regarding the quarrels

פ. פתח להיות עומד ומתפלל
He opened [himself] to stand and to be engaged in prayer.

פ, צ. פסלים, צלמים
idols, figures

ק. קודם מתן תורה
Prior to the giving of the Torah.

ר. רחום בדין
Merciful in judgment

ש. שערי חצרות, שערי מדינות, שערי עירות
gates of courtyards, gates of states, gates of cities

ת. תפילין שבזרוע, תפילין שבראש
Tefillin on the arm, Tefillin on the head

Questions

א משה promised בני ישראל that _____ was not like _____, but _____; and _____, which was _____, still _____. (11:10)

ב What kind of ברכה is ואכלת ושבעת? (11:15)

ג Hashem tells בני ישראל that if they begin a מצוה, "_____". (8:1)

ד ארץ ישראל is a land that ה' _____, which means that through it, _____. (11:12)

ה _____ forgave בני ישראל on יום _____ for the חטא _____; therefore this day was _____. (9:18)

ו Two examples of how the תורה recounts two of the signs that ה' performed for בני ישראל in מצרים. (7:19)

ז ארץ ישראל produces _____. (8:8)

ח בני ישראל were expected to view the מצות as _____. (11:13)

ט Which expression did משה use to describe that the golden calf was being ground even to this present day? (9:21)

י בני ישראל were told that if they keep the מצות then ה' _____. (7:12)

כ, ל The _____ were given the job _____ and the _____ were given the tasks _____ and _____ through נשיאות _____. (10:8)

מ, נ The _____ refer to the _____ ה' performed for בני ישראל in מצרים. (7:19)

ס, ע _____ refers to someone who leaves the ways of תורה, which then leads to his clinging to _____. (11:16)

פ _____ refers to a fear which is _____. (11:25)

צ A type of flying insect that would shoot bile. (7:20)

ק What did משה demonstrate by connecting the events of breaking the לוחות to the death of אהרן? (10:7)

ר What did the Rabbis learn from the fact that משה told בני ישראל that all they are expected to do is to fear ה'? (10:12)

ש One of the ברכות that בני ישראל would receive is that there would be no one from amongst them _____. (7:14)

ת What did משה demand of בני ישראל to know? (11:2)

Answers

א. ארץ ישראל, ארץ מצרים, אלא טובה הימנה, אפילו ארץ רעמסס אשר ישבתם בה, ארץ מצרים, אף היא אינה כארץ ישראל

Eretz Yisrael, Eretz Mitzrayim, rather it is better than [Mitzrayim], even the land of Ramses where you settled, Eretz Mitzrayim, even that land is not like Eretz Yisrael

ב. ברכה מצויה בפת בתוך המעים

A blessing found in bread as it is in the stomach.

ג. גמור אותה

finish it

ד. דרש אותה תמיד, דורש את כל הארצות עמה

seeks [out] consistently, [He] consistently seeks out all the lands with it

ה. הקדוש ברוך הוא, הכפורים, העגל, הקבע למחילה ולסליחה

Hakadosh Baruch Hu, [day] of atonement, the calf, was designated for [a day of] forgiveness and pardon

ו. ויהי לנחש, והיו לדם ביבשת

it became a snake, and it turned to blood on dry land

ז. זתים העושים שמן

olives that produce oil

ח. חדשים כאלו שמעתם בו ביום

new [concepts] as if you heard them [for the first time] today

ט. טחון

grinding

י. ישמר לך הבטחתו

[He] will keep His promise to you

כ, ל. לוים, לשאת את הארון, כהנים, לעמד לפני ה' לשרתו, לברך בשמו, כפיים

Leviim, carry the Ark, Kohanim, stand in front of Hashem to service Him, Bless [the Jewish people] in His name, hands

מ, נ. מסת, נסיונות

outstanding signs, miraculous feats

ס, ע. סרתם, עבודה זרה

veered [off the path], idolatry

פ. פחד, פתאום

fear, sudden

צ. צרעה

tziraah

ק. קשה מיתתן של צדיקים לפני הקדוש ברוך הוא

The day upon which a righteous person dies is very difficult for Hakadosh Baruch Hu.

ר. רבותינו דרשו מכאן הכל בידי שמים חוץ מיראת שמים

Our Rabbis learn from here that everything is in the hands of Heaven except for the fear of Heaven.

ש. שאינו מוליד

that cannot father children

ת. תנו לב לדעת ולהבין ולקבל תוכחתי

"Give heart to your knowledge in order to know and comprehend and accept my rebuke".

Questions

א These words demonstrate that עבודה זרה must be completely destroyed and uprooted. (12:2)

א An _____ is an _____ and therefore must be burned down. (12:3)

ב What is a pillar made of one stone called, in the משנה? (12:3)

ג It is prohibited for someone to make a _____ on one's skin to mourn a dead person because בני ישראל, the children of ה', should look nice and not _____. (14:1)

ד A false prophet is killed because he _____, which is _____. (13:6)

ה Someone who worships עבודה זרה, _____, and חז"ל say that _____. (11:28)

ו, ז The תורה says _____ regarding preparation of the קרבן פסח; _____. (16:7)

ח One of the signs of a כשר animal. (14:6)

ח, ט There are more _____ than בהמות _____. (14:4–5)

י When the עבד עברי is set free, one is supposed to give him animals from his herd, but _____. (15:14)

כ What is the effect of עבודה זרה on the world? (13:18)

ל The bread eaten on פסח is called _____ because it is _____. (16:3)

מ Which place is referred to as the resting place of ה'? (12:5)

נ What served as a sign to בני ישראל that they can successfully conquer ארץ ישראל? (11:31)

ס, ע The תורה instructs us to open our hands and give money to _____ even if this means getting any of them a _____ or an _____. (15:8)

ע Why is the eighth day of סכות referred to as עצרת? (16:8)

פ One is allowed to use _____ as סכך for the סוכה. (16:13)

צ What can we learn from the fact that the תורה says one will be rewarded for refraining from eating the blood of an animal? (12:25)

ק The תורה says that בני ישראל is a nation that is _____, which means that they should _____. (14:21)

ר, ש הר עיבל and הר גריזים were located _____, next to _____. (11:30)

ת Which מצות are בני ישראל instructed to listen to? (13:5)

Answers

א. אבד תאבדון

destroy you shall destroy

א. אשרה, אילן הנעבד

Asheira, a tree which was worshiped as idolatry

ב. בימוס

bimos

ג. גדידה ושרט, גדודים ומקורחים

cut and a scratch, cut up or bald

ד. דבר סרה, דבר המוסר מן העולם

spoke lies, something removed from this world

ה. הרי הוא סר מכל הדרך, המודה בעבודה זרה כבופר בכל התורה כלה

he has strayed from the entire path, one who gives recognition to idolatry is considered as if he denies the entire Torah

ו, ז. ובשלת, זהו צלי אש שאף הוא קרוי בישול

"you shall cook it," this is roasting on the fire because even roasting is referred to as cooking

ח. חלוקה בשתי צפרנים

split in two of its hooves

ח, ט. חיות טמאות, טהורות

impure animals, pure

י. יצאו פרדות

excluding mules

כ. כל זמן שעבודה זרה בעולם חרון אף בעולם

As long as there is idolatry in the world there will be anger in the world.

ל. לחם עוני, לחם שמזכיר את העוני

bread of affliction, bread that reminds us of [our] affliction

מ. משכן שילה

[The] Tabernacle of Shilo

נ. נסים של ירדן

Miracles of the Jordan

ס, ע. עניים, סוס לרכוב עליו, עבד לרוץ לפניו

poor people, a horse to ride upon, a servant to run before [him]

ע. עצור עצמך מן המלאכה

[On it you should] stop yourself from working.

פ. פסלת גורן ויקב

leftovers of the threshing floor and wine press

צ. צא ולמד מתן שכרן של המצות

Go and learn what reward a person receives for performing Mitzvoth.

ק. קדוש, קדש את עצמך במה שמותר לך

holy, sanctify yourselves by monitoring those matters that are permissible to you

ר, ש. רחוק מן הגלגל, שכם

far away from the Gilgal, Shechem

ת. תורת משה

Torat Moshe

Questions

א A judge cannot take bribery _____. (16:19)

ב How do judges assess witnesses? (19:18)

ג What is the position of the בית המקדש in relation to everyplace else in the world? (17:8)

ה, ד שופטים are _____ and שוטרים are people _____. (16:18)

ו Testimony must be heard from the witnesses, _____, and the judges must understand the language the witnesses are talking, _____. (19:15)

ז People who stood and encouraged בני ישראל to fight and not to flee from battle are known as _____. (20:9)

ח When the תורה refers to matters of dispute, it means that the _____. (17:8)

ט בני ישראל are allowed to slay males during war except for the _____. (20:14)

י When witnesses come to testify, it is crucial that _____. (19:17)

כ What is a person expected to do with the wool from his herd of animals? (18:4)

ל Why is the עגלה ערופה brought? (21:4)

מ A type of person who does not go out to war. (20:1)

מ, נ A _____ should not have more then eighteen _____, as we learn by דוד, who had six _____ and was told that he could add two times more. (17:17)

ס The תורה informs us that if a foreign nation does not attempt to make peace with בני ישראל, _____. (20:12)

ע When the תורה says _____, it is referring to a monetary payment for damages. (19:21)

פ Someone who was not _____ his _____ on the fourth year returns home and cannot go out to war. (20:6)

צ An example of an event that a מנחש bases his decisions upon. (18:10)

ק What kind of place is נחל איתן? (21:4)

ר A judge has to be careful not to be _____. (16:19)

ש _____ can result from someone feeling _____ toward someone else. (19:11)

ת The נחלה of the כהנים and לוים. (18:1)

Answers

א. אפילו לשפוט צדק

even to judge righteously

ב. בדרישה ובחקירה

through asking and investigation

ג. גבוה מכל המקומות

higher than all other places

ד, ה. דיינים הפוסקים את הדין, הרודין את העם

judges who decide the law, who impose authority over the nation

ו. ולא שיכתבו עדותם באגרת, ולא שיעמוד תורגמן

and [the witnesses] are not allowed to write their testimony down on paper, and [the witnesses] are not allowed to place an interpreter in their stead

ז. זקפין

people who stand upright

ח. חכמי העיר חולקין בדבר

the wise men of the city are divided regarding the matter

ט. טף

children

י. יהיה דומה להם כאלו עומדין לפני המקום

they should see it as if they were standing in front of Hashem

כ. כשאתה גוזז צאנך בכל שנה תן ממנה ראשית לכהן

Every year when you sheer the wool from your flock give the first part of [the wool] to the Kohen.

ל. לכפר על הריגתו של זה שלא הניחוהו לעשות פירות

To atone for the murder of this person who was not left to make his own fruit [bear children].

מ. מחוסר אבר

[one who is] missing a limb

מ, נ. מלך, נשים, נשים

king, wives, wives

ס. סופה להלחם בך

in the end they will wage war with you

ע. עין בעין

an eye for an eye

פ. פודה, פירות

redeem, fruit

צ. צבי הפסיקו בדרך

[a] deer blocks him in the road

ק. קשה שלא נעבד

hard [land] that has not been worked

ר. רך לזה וקשה לזה

lenient regarding one person and harsh regarding another person

ש. שפיכות דמים, שנאה

murder, hatred

ת. תרומות ומעשרות

Trumot Umaasrot

Questions

א The תורה warns that when one uses _____ for weights and measures in business, he should use _____ because _____. The תורה also warns against being dishonest with weights and measures because _____. (25:14)

ב What kind of מלחמה is the תורה referring to at the beginning of the פרשה? (21:10)

ג What is a מעקה? (22:8)

ד A woman is not allowed to wear men's clothing in order to be _____. (22:5)

ה The תורה prohibits having a donkey and ox plow together, and _____. (22:10)

ו From these words we learn that one does not receive מלקות while standing or sitting, but only when bent over in a leaning position. (25:2)

ז What should someone do if tempted to speak לשון הרע? (24:9)

ח Where was considered outside of the camp of בני ישראל? (23:13)

ט When afflicted with צרעת, one is not allowed to remove any of the signs of _____ that may appear. (24:8)

י The תורה instructs the בית דין to kill the rebellious son when he is still young so that _____. (21:18)

כ Why does the beautiful woman who was taken captive have to sit and cry over her parents for thirty days? (21:13)

ל What do we learn from the fact that the תורה permitted one to marry a woman from a foreign nation who was taken captive? (21:11)

מ During the process of חליצה, there is a _____. (25:10)

נ What type of language does the תורה use to describe something that is off-limits, whether for positive or negative reasons? (22:9)

ס A rebellious son is called _____ because he is _____. (21:18)

ע When בני ישראל came out of מצרים, they were _____. (25:18)

פ, צ Someone who is newly wed to any woman, _____, does not have to go out to the _____, nor does he have to be involved in anything which is _____. (24:5)

ק, ר The process of חליצה involves removing one's shoe from his _____ and spitting on the _____ in front of him. (25:9)

ש During the harvest, you are allowed to eat from the grapes of your friend's vineyard _____, but not a gross amount of eating. (23:25)

ת What does the beautiful woman who is taken captive have to do with her nails and why? (21:12)

Answers

א. אבנים, אבן שלמה וצדק, אם עשית כן יהיה לך הרבה, אם עשית כן לא
יהיה לך כלום

stones, a perfect and just stone, if you do so you will [benefit from having] a lot, if
you do so you will have nothing

ב. במלחמת רשות הכתוב מדבר

The verse refers to an optional war.

ג. גדר מסביב לגג

A fence surrounding [the] roof

ד. דומה לאיש

likened to a man

ה. הוא הדין לכל שני מינים שבעולם

such is the law regarding any two species in the world

ו. והפילו השפט

The judge casts him down.

ז. זכור העשוי למרים

Remember what was done to Miriam.

ח. חוץ לענן

outside the cloud

ט. טומאה

impurity

י. ימות זכאי ואל ימות חייב

he should die innocent and not die guilty

כ. כדי שתהא בת ישראל שמחה וזו עצבה

So that the daughter of Israel should be happy and this girl should be sad.

ל. לא דברה תורה אלא כנגד יצר הרע

The Torah spoke only contest the evil inclination.

מ. מצוה על כל העומדים שם לומר חלוץ נעל

[it is a] Mitzvah for all those present to say "remove your shoe"

נ. נופל בו לשון קדוש

Forms of the word Kiddush apply to it.

ס. סורר ומורה, סר מן הדרך

wayward and rebellious, strayed from the path

ע. עיף בצמא

worn out from thirst

פ, צ. פרט למחזיר גרושתו, צבא, צורך הצבא

except for someone who remarries the woman whom he had divorced, army, [for the] needs of the army

ק, ר. קרקע, רגל

ground, leg

ש. שבער

[to] your satisfaction

ת. תגדלם כדי שתתנול

[She] grows them in order that she will look ugly.

Questions

א, ב _____ were instructed to take _____ and write the words of the תורה on them _____, which means _____. (27:8)

ג Someone who moves back the _____, which means that he _____ of his friend, is cursed. (27:17)

ד The _____ that ארץ ישראל would be blessed with is _____. (26:2)

ה When בני ישראל reminded משה that they stood at סיני and accepted the תורה, then משה was happy, as he responded by telling them, _____ and _____. (29:3)

ו This word means that under certain circumstances, בני ישראל could be completely destroyed and removed. (28:63)

ז Which place is the תורה referring to when it says that ה׳ will bring us אל המקום הזה? (26:9)

ח If ה׳ punishes בני ישראל, what kind of heart will they have? (28:65)

ט This word refers to fruit. (28:5)

י One of the punishments that בני ישראל can receive is that _____ all their crops, which means _____. (28:42)

כ This describes someone who anticipates salvation that never comes. (28:65)

ל, מ When one offers the ביכורים he is _____ by mentioning how _____ and ה׳ destroyed him for contemplating such a plan. (26:5)

נ A person's flesh becomes _____ and _____ if he has שחפת. (28:22)

ס, ע Someone who does not know about a matter is considered _____ and prohibited from directing his friend on the matter because he will be offering an _____. (27:18)

ע בני ישראל were not obligated to offer ביכורים, _____. (26:1)

פ One is obligated to offer ביכורים _____ and not _____. (26:3)

צ If בני ישראל do not follow the words of ה', then foreign nations will be _____, causing tragic circumstances. (28:53)

ק This type of sickness refers to a very high burning fever. (28:22)

ר, ש ביכורים are offered from _____, but not all fruits that are _____ are offered – only fruits which are from _____. (26:2)

ת What is one supposed to do with regard to offering the לוי, convert, orphan and widow to eat from his fields? (26:12)

כי תבא

Answers

א, ב. בני ישראל, אבנים, באר היטב, בשבעים לשון
Bnei Yisrael, stones, explained well, in seventy languages

ג. גבול רעהו, גונב את הקרקע
boundary of his friend, stole the land

ד. דבש, דבש תמרים
honey, date honey

ה. היום הזה נהיית לעם, היום הזה הבנתי שאתם דבקים וחפצים במקום
on this day you have become a nation, on this day I understand that you desire to cling to Hashem

ו. ונסחתם
You will be torn

ז. זה בית המקדש
This is [referring to] the Beit Hamikdash.

ח. חרד
frightened

ט. טנאך
your basket

י. יירש הצלצל, יעשנו הארבה רש מן הפרי
the locust will impoverish, the locust will destroy the fruit

כ. כליון עינים
longing of eyes

ל, מ. מזכיר חסדי המקום, לבן בקש לעקור את הכל
[he] mentions Hashem's kindness, Lavan wanted to uproot everything [whole Jewish Nation]

נ. נשחף, נפוח
worn away, swollen

כי תבא

ס, ע. סומא בדבר, עצה רעה

blind to it, bad advice

ע. עד שכבשו את הארץ וחלקוה

until they would conquer the land and apportion it

פ. פעם אחת בשנה, פעמיים

one time a year, twice

צ. צרים על העיר

threatening to the city

ק. קדחת

an illness

ר, ש. ראשית כל פרי אדמה, ראשית, שבעת המינים

[the] first of all fruits of the ground, first, the seven species [of Eretz Yisrael]

ת. תן להם כדי שבען

Give to them until they are satisfied.

Questions

א The תורה is not in the heavens because _____. (30:12)

ב In what format was the תורה given to בני ישראל? (30:14)

ג משה called עבודה זרה _____ because it was detestable like _____. (29:16)

ד ה׳ expects the Jewish people to carry out _____ on the individual who deserves to be punished. (29:28)

ה When בני ישראל heard all of the curses that will befall them if they do not follow the תורה, _____, so משה reassured them, saying, _____. (29:12)

ו משה addressed those who were in front of him, _____, which includes _____. (29:14)

ז, ח, ט ה׳ offered בני ישראל both _____ and _____, which means that _____: if they do _____, then they will receive _____. (30:15)

י The גוים hid away their idols because they were _____. (29:16)

כ Why did משה say to בני ישראל that they would "pass through" a covenant with ה׳? (29:11)

ל משה assured בני ישראל that ה׳ would be _____ and reinforced this by adding, _____. (29:12)

מ, נ What does the word_____, which means "standing," come to teach us? (29:9)

ס, ע If בני ישראל do not follow the תורה then their land will be destroyed just like _____ and _____.

ע What did משה do with בני ישראל before he died? (29:13)

פ ה׳ made בני ישראל swear to keep the תורה _____. (29:17)

צ, ק As a result of the _____ of _____, ה׳ _____.

ר When משה refers to _____, he is actually referring to one group of people: _____. (29:9)

ש The _____ is _____, and when בני ישראל are redeemed, we know _____. (30:3)

ת ה׳ told בני ישראל that if they follow Him, _____ and if they do not, _____. (30:19)

Answers

א. אלו היתה בשמים היית צריך לעלות אחריה וללמדה
were it in the Heavens you would have to ascend after it and learn it

ב. בכתב ובעל פה
In written [form] and orally.

ג. גלליהם, גלל
[their] idols [derogatory], excrement

ד. דין
judgment

ה. הוריקו פניהם ואמרו מי יוכל לעמוד באלו, הרבה הכעסתם למקום ולא
עשה אתכם כליה והרי אתם קיימים לפניו
their faces grew pale and they said "Who could possibly stand these conditions?";
"You have angered Hashem many times but He did not destroy you – you are still
here alive in front of Him"

ו. ואת אשר איננו פה, ואף עם דורות העתידים להיות
and also those who are not here, [and] even with those from the future genera-
tions

ז, ח, ט. חיים, טוב, זה תלוי בזה, טוב, חיים
life, good, one is dependent on the other, good, life

י. יראים שמא יגנבו
[they were] afraid perhaps they would be stolen

כ. כך היו כורתין ברית עושין מחיצה מכאן ומחיצה מכאן ועוברים בינתים
This is the way a covenant was forged; they would make a wall on each side and
the parties involved would walk between them.

ל. לך לאלהים, לפי שדבר לך ונשבע לאבותיך
your God, as He said to you and promised your forefathers

מ, נ. נצבים, מלמד שכנסם משה לפני הקדוש ברוך הוא ביום מותו להכניסם בברית

[you are] standing, teaches us that Moshe assembled [Bnei Yisrael] in front of Hakadosh Baruch Hu on the day of his death to bring them into a covenant.

ס, ע. סדום, עמורה

Sdom, Amora

ע. עשה אותם מצבה כדי לזרזם

[He] made them stand in front of him in order to exhort them.

פ. פן יש בכם איש או אשה או משפחה או שבט אשר לבבו פנה היום מעם יהוה אלהינו ללכת לעבד את אלהי הגוים ההם

perhaps there is among you a man or a woman or a family or tribe whose heart turns astray from Hashem our God to go and worship a god from those nations

צ, ק. קושי, קיבוץ גליות, צריך להיות אוחז בידיו ממש איש איש ממקומו

hardships, ingathering of the exiles, has to hold each individual's hand in [his or her] specific location

ר. ראשיכם שבטיכם, ראשיכם לשבטיכם

their heads their tribes, [their] heads of their tribes

ש. שכינה, שרויה עם ישראל בצרת גלותם, שהוא ישוב עמהם

the Divine presence of Hashem, dwelling among Bnei Yisrael during the hardships of their exile, that [He] will return with them

ת. תקבלו שכר, תקבלו עונש

[they] will receive reward, [they] will receive punishment

Questions

א What did משה mean when he said that he cannot go in and out anymore? (31:2)

ב The response after a _____ which was recited in the _____ was _____. (32:3)

ג ה׳ reminded משה that he and אהרן could not go into ארץ ישראל because "_____" and "_____" when they hit the rock in front of בני ישראל. (32:51)

ד How were the לוחות situated next to the ארון? (31:26)

ה What did משה inform בני ישראל regarding his age? (31:2)

ו, ז With the words _____, what was משה saying? (31:2)

ח בני ישראל were told that תורה is _____. (32:47)

ט, י ה׳ told _____ that he may have to _____ in order to direct בני ישראל. (31:7)

כ Why did ה׳ instruct משה to ascend and see ארץ ישראל before he died? (32:52)

ל The men came to הקהל _____, the woman came _____, and the children came _____. (31:12)

מ What did משה compare the תורה to which is everlasting? (32:2)

נ A word which always refers to anger. (31:20)

ס, ע During the מצוה of הקהל, the king would stand on a platform of _____ that had been made in the _____, as explained in tractate _____. (31:11)

פ The _____ ripen faster then all the _____. (32:13)

צ What did משה teach בני ישראל with regard to adhering to the words of תורה? (32:46)

ק Two words that mean burning (with anger). (32:21,22)

ר Drops of rain. (32:2)

ש Which promise did ה׳ make to בני ישראל regarding תורה? (31:21)

ת What can be said regarding the relationship between משה and יהושע? (31:29)

וילך־האזינו

Answers

א. איני רשאי שנטלה ממני הרשות ונתנה ליהושע
I am not permitted for the authority has been taken from me and given to Yehoshua.

ב. ברכה, בית המקדש, ברוך שם כבוד מלכותו לעולם ועד
blessing, Beit Hamikdash, "Blessed is the name of the glory of His kingdom forever"

ג. גרמתם למעול בי, גרמתם לי שלא אקדש
you caused others to disgrace Me, you caused Me not to be sanctified

ד. דף היה בולט מן הארון מבחוץ
There was a board protruding from the outside of the Ark.

ה. היום מלאו ימי ושנותי
Today [I completed] my days and years.

ו, ז. ויהוה אמר אלי, זהו פירוש לא אוכל עוד לצאת ולבוא לפי שה אמר אלי
and Hashem said to me, this is the explanation: "I can no longer enter and exit because Hashem told me so"

ח. חייכם
"your lives"

ט, י. יהושע, טול מקל והך על קדקדן
Yehoshua, take a staff and tap it on their heads

כ. כי ידעתי כי חביבה היא לך
Because I know that it is dear to you

ל. ללמוד, לשמוע, לתת שכר למביאיהן
to learn, to hear, to give reward to those who bring them

מ. מטר
rain

218

נ. נאוץ

anger

ס, ע. עץ, עזרה, סוטה

wood, hall, Sotah

פ. פירות ארץ ישראל, פירות הארצות

fruits of Eretz Yisrael, fruits of [other] lands

צ. צריך אדם שיהיו עיניו ואזניו ולבו מכונים לדברי תורה

One must prepare his eyes, ears, and heart to concentrate on the words of Torah.

ק. קנאוני, קדחה

My anger, burned

ר. רביבים

droplets of rain that fall like arrows from the sky

ש. שאין תורה משתבחת מזרעם לגמרי

That the Torah will never be completely forgotten by their offspring.

ת. תלמידו של אדם חביב עליו כגופו

One's student is as endeared to him as his [very] self.

וזאת הברכה

Questions

א What is the נגב? (34:3)

ב How did משה die? (34:5)

ג Which ברכה was given to יוסף that means that the fruits on his land will always replenish themselves? (33:14)

ד One of the battles that ה׳ showed משה before he died was _____. (34:2)

ה, ו From the words _____, we learn that ה׳ offered the תורה to בני עשו first but they did not want it; and from the words _____, we learn that ה׳ offered the תורה to בני ישמעאל as well and they did not want it. (33:2)

ז שבט דן will split into two areas just like _____. (33:22)

ח, ט יששבר and זבולון will be blessed with _____, such as _____ and _____, which come from the sea and the _____. (33:19)

י Which famous body of water was in נפתלי's portion? (33:23)

כ משה described how by סיני, ה׳ greeted His people _____. (33:2)

ל When משה died, _____ and _____, which means that the _____ and _____. (34:7)

מ What did משה say after he specified the ברכות that בני ישראל would receive? (33:29)

נ How did ה׳ demonstrate His greatness to בני ישראל? (34:12)

ס When did משה actually offer his ברכה to בני ישראל and why? (33:1)

ע יששכר and זבולון _____ whereby זבולון would work while יששכר were _____. (33:18)

פ When משה offered his ברכה to בני ישראל, _____ and afterward _____. (33:1)

וזאת הברכה

צ The souls of _____ are hidden away with ה׳ and the righteousness of בני ישראל clings to ה׳ and He protects them. (33:3)

ק יהושע was _____ like the strength of an ox and beautiful like the _____. (33:17)

ר When אהרן died both men and women mourned because he was _____. (34:8)

ש What kind of relationship did משה have with ה׳? (34:10)

ת Something which בני ישראל held on to and will never abandon. (33:4)

Answers

א. ארץ הדרום

land of the South

ב. בנשיקה

with a kiss [from Hashem]

ג. גרש ירחים

the moon's yield

ד. דבורה ובלק נלחמים

Devorah and Balak engaged in war

ה, ו. וזרח משעיר למו, הופיע מהר פארן

and [He] shone forth to them from Seir, [He] appeared [to them] from Mount Paran

ז. זנוק זה יוצא ממקום אחד ונחלק לשני מקומות

[a] spring begins to flow from one place and is split into two places

ח, ט. טמוני חול, טרית, חלזון, חול

hidden in sand, tuna, chilazon [snail], sand

י. ים כנרת

Kineret Sea

כ. כחתן היוצא להקביל פני כלה

like a groom goes out to meet his bride

ל. לא כהתה עינו, לא נס לחה, לחלוחית שבו לא שלט בו רקבון, לא נהפך תואר פניו

his eyes did not dim, his [body's] moisture did not leave him, the liquids in his body did not cause decay, the countenance of his face did not change

מ. מה לי לפרוט לכם כלל דבר הכל שלכם

"Why do I need to specify for you all the matters, overall all is yours".

נ. ניסים וגבורות שבמדבר הגדול והנורא

Miracles and strength demonstrated in the vast and awesome desert.

ס. סמוך למיתתו שאם לא עכשיו אימתי

Right before his death – because if not now, then when?

ע. עשו שתפות, עוסקים בתורה

made a partnership, immersed in [studying] Torah

פ. פתח תחילה בשבחו של מקום, פתח בצרכיהם של ישראל

[he] opened first by praising Hashem, opened regarding the needs of Yisrael

צ. צדיקים

the righteous

ק. קשה, קרני ראם

tough, ram's horns

ר. רודף שלום

pursued peace

ש. שהיה לבו גס בו

His heart was coarse with Him [they had an informal relationship].

ת. תורה

Torah